New Orleans
Yesterday and Today

New Orleans
Yesterday and Today

 A GUIDE TO THE CITY

Third Edition

WALTER G. COWAN   CHARLES L. DUFOUR

JOHN C. CHASE   O. K. LEBLANC

                           JOHN WILDS

LOUISIANA STATE UNIVERSITY PRESS

BATON ROUGE

Copyright © 1983 by Louisiana State University Press
New material copyright © 1988, 2001 by Louisiana State University Press
All rights reserved
Manufactured in the United States of America

Designer: Joanna Hill
Typeface: Linotron Garamond #3
Typesetter: G&S Typesetters, Inc.

Louisiana Paperback Edition, 1983; Revised Edition, 1988; Third Edition, 2001
02 04 06 08 10 09 07 05 03 01
2 4 5 3 1

Library of Congress Cataloging-in-Publication Data

New Orleans yesterday and today : a guide to the city / Walter G. Cowan ... [et al.].—3rd ed.
    p. cm.
    Includes index
    ISBN 0-8071-2743-4 (alk. paper)
    1. New Orleans (La.)—Description and travel. 2. New Orleans (La.)—Guidebooks. 3.
New Orleans (La.)—History. I. Cowan, Walter G.

F379.N54 N48 2001
917.63'350464—dc21

                                                                          2001029683

The paper in this book meets the guidelines for permanence and durability of
the Committee on Production Guidelines for Book Longevity of the Council on
Library Resources. ∞

 CONTENTS

Part II The People and Their History

Part III The Flavor of the City

❧ ILLUSTRATIONS ❧

⚜ PREAMBLE ⚜

The Battle of New Orleans freed America once and for all from European domination. The capture of the city by a Federal fleet doomed the southern Confederacy, assuring that the United States would remain an undivided republic destined to become a world power.

Into these historic surroundings the Republican party chose to bring its 1988 national convention. It was more than the lure of the past, however, that impelled the Grand Old Party to pick its presidential nominee in the Louisiana Superdome. The site selection committee was also motivated by the fact that as a convention city New Orleans has advantages that cannot be matched by any other metropolis.

Beginning with facilities, no other structure in the country equals the Superdome, where up to 80,000 persons can be seated in a vast arena fitted with modern television and public-address conveniences. The Superdome is the focal point for such events as political conventions, but for business and professional meetings and for trade shows, the center of activity can be switched to the riverfront and the New Orleans Convention Center, one of the world's largest.

How many other American cities can offer more than 35,000 hotel rooms? And where else, except perhaps in New York and San Francisco, is there such an array of world-class restaurants and such unique and distinguished cuisine?

Sightseeing and shopping? The centerpiece is the French Quarter, a relic of eighteenth-century France and Spain. It is one of America's prized tourist attractions. But there is also Mark Twain's Mississippi River. Paddle-wheel packets are there for excursions. On the bank are the Riverwalk and Jax Brewery, where scores of retail stores offer their goods in exciting settings.

The key word is proximity, as the hundreds of thousands who have come to New Orleans for Mardi Gras, Super Bowl football games, Final Four basketball tournaments, and world championship prize-fights have learned. Most of the hotels are situated in the central business district, and from any of these the Superdome, the French Quarter, the riverfront, the Convention Center, and most of the other attractions, including a world-class aquarium, are within walking distance.

❧ AUTHORS' NOTE ❧

We, the authors of this book, developed such a love affair with New Orleans that we decided to tell the city's history as we knew it. So we ask the indulgence of our readers if some of our affection for New Orleans shows. Nevertheless, we have tried to be objective, pointing out its foibles as well as its charms.

Our book has a fourfold purpose:

(1) To treat New Orleans' colorful history, not in a chronological order, but in a topical way, with each chapter, while integrated into the whole, standing as an individual essay; (2) To capture in words and drawings the international flavor and the unique feel of our many-faceted city; (3) To provide visitors to the city with a book, convenient in size and scope, which will tell them what to see and how to go about seeing it; (4) To offer New Orleanians a "refresher course" in their city's past and present and to remind them that being "already here" is, indeed, a rare privilege.

We acknowledge with gratitude the contributions much beyond the call of duty of Barbara Phillips and Marie Blanchard of the Louisiana State University Press; Stanton M. Frazar and Pat McWhorter of the Historic New Orleans Collection; Collin P. Hamer, Jr., of the New Orleans Public Library; and Jane Stevens of the Howard-Tilton Memorial Library, Tulane.

New Orleans
Yesterday and Today

❧ PREFACE ❧

New Orleans, a centuries-old American city enriched by its European heritage and noted for its culture, cuisine, and entertainment as well as its status as a world port, moved into the twenty-first century determined to build on its legacy.

Founded in 1718 at the point of a crescent in the rapidly flowing Mississippi River, a spot suggested by Indians native to the area, the city quickly developed into a port with significant commerce from the Mississippi Valley, which would send goods downriver and beyond, into the open sea. But not until the invention of the steamboat nearly a century later did the port begin to fulfill its potential, since it could then ship upstream as well as downstream.

In the meantime, the original French settlers built a city in the image of their mother country. That original section, known as the Vieux Carré (Old Square), or more popularly as the French Quarter, is a six-by-eleven-block retangle that has retained its charm and become a magnet for tourists. After some forty-five years of French rule, the Louisiana colony was ceded to Spain, and the influence of the Spanish—in customs and architecture, especially—soon became evident and remains today. Though built primarily by French and Spanish settlers, the city was later infused with the energy of thousands of people from other European countries plus many others from Latin America, Africa, and Asia.

This painting by Marie Adrien Persac illustrates how the New Orleans port looked just before the Civil War. As you can see, it was a stronghold of activity and a prize

for Union forces who captured it in April of 1862. Courtesy Historic New Orleans Collection. A Clarisse Claiborne Grima Acquisition Fund Purchase.

It is also a city that has suffered through both an attempted revolt when France relinquished control and two wars, with its citizens fighting the British in the Battle of New Orleans in 1815 and Union troops in 1860–64 during the Civil War.

New Orleans took on a special character as it flourished through the eighteenth, nineteenth, and twentieth centuries, and was recognized as the queen city of the South in the mid-1800s, when with a population of 155,000, it was the fifth largest city in the United States. (By the year 2000, however, it had long since lost its high numerical rank; nevertheless, it was home to some half-million residents amid a metropolitan population of 1,316,510.)

Situated almost ninety miles from the mouth of the Mississippi River, it was natural that the port would quickly become the vital link between the Mississippi Valley and the rest of the world—so important, in fact, that President Thomas Jefferson in 1803 engineered the Louisiana Purchase, buying not just New Orleans but the entire Louisiana Territory for his United States. Historians point out that the land now occupied by the U.S. might have become three separate nations had not Jefferson acted precipitously, ignoring legalities presented by the Constitution that required congressional approval for such an action. His quick decision headed off the possibility of the eastern coast becoming a British entity, with France ruling the Mississippi Valley and Spain ruling what is now our West.

People seem never to tire of viewing the Mississippi River and the traffic it generates, from the chugging tugboats to the ferries, the tankers and freighters to the sleek cruise ships.

History has been written in the downtown levee area of New Orleans. It was here that the fleet of Captain (later Admiral) David Farragut anchored after steaming up the Mississippi to conquer the city on April 25, 1862, during the Civil War. The Union fleet was greeted by a scene of great devastation: New Orleans' defenders had set ships afire to prevent their seizure and burned the cotton, tobacco, sugar, corn, and rice piled on the levees. Molasses was poured into the streets, and warehouses emptied of all foodstuffs. Almost fifty years earlier, from a vantage point in the area, residents could hear and see action in the Battle of New Orleans, fought at Chalmette on January 8, 1815.

Throughout most of the 1800s, the harbor scene was that of dozens of schooners, steamboats, barges, and other vessels loading or unloading cargo. Writing in 1854 in *The Homes of the New World: Impressions of America,* Frederica Bremer stated, "Tyre, nor Carthage, Alexandria nor Genoa, those fore time metroples of merchant princes, boasted no quay like the levee of New Orleans." Robert C. Reinders, in his book *End of an Era: New Orleans in 1850–60,* perhaps told the story more aptly when he wrote: "The heart of New Orleans' economic life in the ante-bellum period rested on the waterfront; almost the entire economy directly or indirectly was related to activity on the thin line of wharves and levees which rimmed the Mississippi."

From a historical perspective, an inhabitant of or visitor to this mostly below-sea-level city might well conclude that New Orleans' uniqueness sets it apart from the average American city. While this book was written with that quality in mind, and to celebrate the Louisiana World Exposition (World's Fair) of 1984, the book's popularity as a historical reference and guide has given it an extended life. Thus, this updated third edition.

The 1984 World's Fair, and one a century earlier held on a site that became Audubon Park, were financial failures, but each proved to be a catalyst for economic progress. The more recent event literally changed the face and character of the Canal Street–riverfront area and the Central Business District. In anticipation of the crowds, a railroad switching yard and station became the site of a major hotel development (the Hilton), and this location, also an area of large docks and warehouses where goods destined for overseas shipment were stored, later became the site of the 1984 World's Fair.

The building of a 1,100,000-square-foot convention center,

The New Orleans Convention Center, on the site of the 1984 Louisiana World Exposition. Courtesy New Orleans Convention Center.

used as a great hall during the fair, started a movement to attract large conventions and trade shows. Significant expansion of the center soon put New Orleans in a position to hold most of the nation's largest meetings.

The city has retained its uniqueness as it has transformed architecturally appealing old department stores and historic commercial structures into fancy, upscale hotels. Colorful streetcars that ran the Canal Street route, which was abandoned in the 1960s, are being brought back, and they are already running along the riverfront. An arts complex, including the Ogden Museum emphasizing southern artworks, the D-Day Museum honoring the soldiers of World War II, and even a major gambling casino (Harrah's) have been built to embellish the area.

Here the new blends with the old in a city determined to preserve its past. And a past it has, evidenced by its struggles through epidemics of yellow fever, cholera, the wars and the politics of the Huey Long and other eras.

But the story of New Orleans isn't just history. It is the frivolity of Mardi Gras, the liveliness of its jazz music, and the desire of practically everyone to taste its cuisine. The place has developed its own personality, culture, and character. It has also become a sports center, having the nation's largest indoor playing facility in the Superdome, where the Sugar Bowl and (frequently) the Super Bowl are played; a new sports arena for basketball, hockey, and other entertainment uses; a stadium that houses a professional baseball team; not to mention a major annual golf tournament. There is also the Aquarium of the Americas—and Jazzland, a new facility devoted to music and family entertainment.

Steeped in history, this old city retains its importance as a shipping center while bolstering its economy by making the most of its past.

W.G.C.

❧ INTRODUCTION ❧

The sun comes up over the west bank of the Mississippi River. Every man can be a king, every woman a queen. The dead are "buried" aboveground. Voodoo practitioners still stick pins into dolls. The bars never close. The telephone directory reads like one in Paris, or in Palermo. Streetcars rumble along tree-shaded streets. You'd swear some of the accents came straight out of Brooklyn. A sidewalk is a "banquette," the median of a divided avenue a "neutral ground."

New Orleans is different, always has been, always will be.

It made no sense in the first place to build a seaport 110 miles from deep water, to site a city on a below-sea-level trembling prairie, alongside a great river that goes on periodic rampages, in a location where hurricanes sometimes howl.

Yet it was Fate, or a stroke of brilliant soothsaying, that caused the youthful Jean-Baptiste Le Moyne, Sieur de Bienville, to pick a spot at a bend in the Mississippi and decree that it would be the capital of the French territory in the heart of America. How could he have sensed that pivotal chapters of the history of the New World would be written on this spot?

New Orleans was unique from that day in 1718 when the first Frenchmen began moving over from earlier settlements at Biloxi and Mobile. The colony was a part of John Law's grandiose project, which contributed to the bankruptcy of France. The inhabitants were reluctant pioneers, many of them criminals or prostitutes exiled from their native land. No dreams of carving an empire out of a wilderness motivated this band.

Louis XV set the stage in 1762 for the first revolt against a European mother country by a colony in the New World. He secretly ceded Louisiana to Spain. In 1768—eight years before the signing of America's Declaration of Independence from England— the French colonists at New Orleans rose up and sent the Spanish governor packing. Five paid with their lives when Alexander O'Reilly, an Irishman in the service of Spain, arrived with an army of 2,600 troops.

New Orleans was the key prize in 1803 when Napoleon Bonaparte, having regained Louisiana for France, completed the biggest real estate transaction in history, the Louisiana Purchase. By acquiring the vast mid-continent area drained by the Mississippi, the young American Republic eliminated a foreign menace on its borders and opened the way for the winning of the West and the realization of a great power's destiny. Few more significant events have occurred in the Western Hemisphere than the lowering of the French flag and the raising of the Stars and Stripes in the Place d'Armes in New Orleans on December 20, 1803.

A nation's fate hung in the balance on January 8, 1815, in the Battle of New Orleans. The War of 1812 had ended, but the armies did not know it. Had General Andrew Jackson not repulsed the British forces on the plains at Chalmette, below New Orleans, the British conceivably could have repudiated the Treaty of Ghent and held New Orleans and exercised control of the Mississippi River.

Half a century later, on April 25, 1862, another event of transcendent importance to the United States occurred at New Orleans. The major city of the Confederacy fell to the Union fleet of Captain David Farragut. The loss, and the blocking of the Mississippi, doomed the Confederacy, although three years would pass before the final surrender. New Orleans knew the indignity of occupation by enemy troops, and later experienced a dozen turbulent years of Reconstruction, marked by a massacre in a meeting hall and a pitched battle on Canal Street with artillery pounding from both sides.

This Monument to General Andrew Jackson by Clark Mills was the first equestrian statue to be produced in the United States. Located in Jackson Square, it was unveiled in 1856, to honor the savior of New Orleans. Photo by A. J. Meek.

The cockeyed compass (*upper right*) plainly shows there are no compass courses in New Orleans, where South Claiborne Avenue runs northwest, where West End is east of East End, and where you drive southeast over two bridges to get to the West Bank. The best way to see New Orleans is to get lost, and its streets seem designed

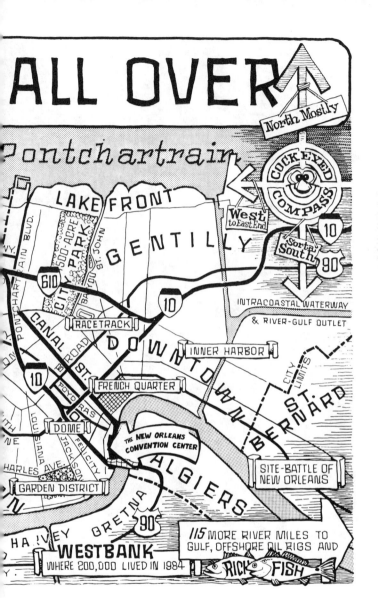

with that in mind. Main directions are uptown and downtown, which are upriver and downriver from Canal Street, and lakefront and west bank, although the last is "sorta south." Map by John C. Chase.

The aboveground tombs in St. Patrick Cemetery, No. 1 and other cemeteries, many whitewashed anew on All Saints' Day, are a distinctive feature of the New Orleans cityscape. Photo by A. J. Meek.

From New Orleans in 1877, former Confederate leaders master-minded the most blatant political deal of the century, manipulating the arrangement that made Rutherford B. Hayes president of the United States in exchange for the withdrawal of occupying troops and the end of Reconstruction.

Out of New Orleans in the last decade of the nineteenth century arose the test case *Plessy* v. *Ferguson*, in which the United States Supreme Court set the doctrine of separate but equal facilities that doomed Negroes to more than a half century of second-class citizenship.

Fires, floods, storms, financial panics beset the city. Cholera wiped out one-tenth of the population in 1832. Pestilence in the form of yellow fever returned again and again, accounting over the years for no less than a hundred thousand deaths. Riots wrote bloody pages in New Orleans history.

Events took strange turns. The priest who tried to introduce the dread Inquisition in New Orleans during the Spanish years returned with a French name to become the most beloved cleric ever to serve the archdiocese.

Bienville's city proved unconquerable. The wharves so far from the sea became the busiest port in America. The boosters for the rockets that launched man on his way to the moon were built in the city. The only art form to originate in America—jazz music—took on a New Orleans beat at its birth in the city.

Through good times and bad, New Orleans developed a personality shaped by diverse influences. French and Spanish colonists, Africans, the Anglo-Saxon Kaintocks, Irish, Germans, Italians, Yugoslavs, they all contributed to the ethos that most Americans find fascinating. By the last quarter of the twentieth century their curiosity resulted in a major source of livelihood for the inhabitants—the tourist and convention industry. At the same time oil and gas production both offshore in the Gulf of Mexico and onshore throughout Louisiana turned the city into an energy center.

New high-rise hotels and office buildings converted the traditional horizontal skyline—once it was thought the soil would support only squat structures—into a vertical one. Yet the nostalgia never vanished. Preservation-minded citizens saw to that. Because of strict laws, the French Quarter remains largely a relic of the colonial period. The older residential neighborhoods also are unchanged. Paddle-wheel steamboats still ply the Mississippi. A resident of the Civil War era would feel at home today in the Jackson Square–St. Louis Cathedral–Cabildo–Pontalba Buildings area, heart of the historic Vieux Carré.

Mardi Gras, a celebration that most Americans associate with New Orleans, finds new generations as eager to participate as were their forebears. The number of organizations—called krewes—has multiplied, and now at least theoretically every man and woman could become a Carnival ruler. A few stores still offer voodoo paraphernalia, and occasionally a clue, such as a pin-pricked doll, suggests that some New Orleanians have not abandoned sorcery. Blue laws never worked in the city, and the partying goes on around the clock. The influx from abroad is represented by the names in the telephone directory. One streetcar line, which runs along the neutral ground of tree-shaded St. Charles Avenue, has not yielded to buses. Some third- and fourth-generation New Orleanians speak with accents that are reminiscent of Brooklyn. Why the similarity, nobody knows.

The original New Orleans nestled in a bend of the mighty Mississippi, hence the appellation Crescent City. Because of the river's meandering, an early riser can stand at the foot of Canal Street and watch the sun come up over Algiers, which is on the west bank of the Mississippi. It is true that the sun eventually sets in the west. Is it too confusing to remind that actually it disappears over the *east* bank of the Mississippi in Jefferson Parish?

J.W.

Part I
The City

1.

⚜ THE RIVER ⚜

If it were not for the Mississippi River, New Orleans would never have been founded. And, if it were not for the river, New Orleans would not have continued to exist since 1718. It was the river that made New Orleans an American city; it was the river, and Spanish restrictions of American use of it, that brought about the greatest real estate deal in history—the Louisiana Purchase.

Because of the Mississippi's deepwater access to the seven seas, New Orleans is the second port in cargo value in the United States. Fifty cents out of every trade dollar in New Orleans comes directly from its port. The Mississippi has been the broad highway down which came prosperity and disaster—commerce and floods—and up which came pestilence and military invasion. Yet, throughout the times of trouble, New Orleans survived and, during the times of plenty, the city prospered because of the Mississippi River.

It is a river of many names supplied by the Indians, the Spanish, and the French. The name Mississippi comes from the Algonquian words *misi*, "great," and *sipi*, "water." From "great water" to Father of Waters is an easy development of Indian imagery. In his authoritative *Louisiana Place Names of Indian Origin*, William A. Read states: "First heard by the early French missionaries and explorers from the lips of the Indians who lived on the upper reaches of the Mississippi, the name came gradually to include the entire course of the river."

New Orleans skyline, showing skyscrapers at the foot of Canal Street, as seen from the West Bank. Photo by A. J. Meek.

While the upriver Indians called their river Mississippi, variously recorded by the French as Mischipi, Messipi, Michasippi, and Missisipi, the Indians encountered by Pierre Le Moyne, Sieur d'Iberville, in 1699 on the lower reaches of the river called it Malbanchia, which had such transcriptions as Malbanchyia, Malabanchia, Balbanchia, and Barbancha. The Spanish names for the Mississippi were Rio Grande, Rio de Spiritu Santo, and Palizado, the last because of mud lumps at the river's mouth that resembled palisades. The French had their names, too, for the Mississippi—Immaculate Conception, Colbert, St. Louis.

The Mississippi stretches some 2,500 miles from its source in Minnesota to its mouth, draining thirty-one states and two Canadian provinces as it meanders down through the Midwest and mid-South. It has a watershed of more than one million square miles, which is one-eighth the area of the continental United States. Its volume is 8 times that of the Rhine and 175 times that of the Thames. In all, it drains 41 percent of the United States. The length of the Mississippi-Missouri system is second only to that of the Nile, which courses more than 3,900 miles. The Mississippi basin is second only to that of the Amazon.

The United States Corps of Engineers has estimated that 300 billion gallons of water flow past New Orleans daily—110 trillion gallons per year—which is more than double the amount used in the United States for all purposes on a given day. In every 1,000 pounds of water, the river carries 2 pounds of dirt, thus deriving its monicker, Muddy Mississippi. Each year, engineers say, the Mississippi pours downstream 670 billion pounds of topsoil, enough to build a pyramid 72 times as large as the Great Pyramid of Egypt, which towers 482 feet from the 755-foot base.

The Spanish were the first Europeans to reach the Mississippi. In 1519, Alvarez de Piñeda, cruising along the Gulf Coast, sighted a great river, which doubtless was the Mississippi. Cabeza de Vaca and three companions, only survivors of Pánfilo de Narváez's expedition of six hundred men that landed in Florida in 1528, encountered the Mississippi as they struggled for years through the wilderness to reach Mexico in 1536.

The first Europeans to travel on the Mississippi were those of Hernando de Soto's expedition. In 1543, after de Soto had died on the banks of the Mississippi, south of present-day Memphis, Luis de Moscoso had boats built to transport the survivors down the river to the Gulf and thence to Mexico.

The French Jesuit missionary Jacques Marquette and the trader-explorer Louis Jolliet paddled down the Mississippi as far south as the Arkansas River in 1673. Nine years later, René Robert Cavelier, Sieur de La Salle, descended the river all the way to the Gulf. On April 9, 1682, La Salle claimed all the land drained by the Mississippi and its tributaries for France, and named it Louisiane in honor of the Sun King, Louis XIV. The vastness of La Salle's claim can be appreciated by considering that it included all the territory between the Alleghenies and the Rockies, an area that extended from 225 miles from the Atlantic Ocean to within 500 miles of the Pacific Ocean.

In 1699, Iberville entered the Mississippi and the settlement of Louisiana was launched. A year less than two decades later, Iberville's younger brother, Jean-Baptiste Le Moyne, Sieur de Bienville, founded New Orleans and the city's long romance with the river, often troubled, began.

Until the disastrous French and Indian War, France controlled the entire Mississippi Valley. But, by the terms of the Treaty of Paris, signed on February 10, 1763, France surrendered Canada and all of Louisiana east of the Mississippi, except New Orleans, to England. Three months earlier, by the secret Treaty of Fontainebleau, signed on November 3, 1762, Louis XV had ceded Louisiana west of the Mississippi and New Orleans to his Bourbon cousin, Charles III of Spain. Spanish authority was not firmly established until 1769. So for practical purposes France had control of the river at New Orleans for fifty-one years.

Between 1769 and November 30, 1803, Spain controlled the Mississippi at New Orleans. On the latter date, Spain transferred Louisiana to France, which held it for only twenty days before transferring it to the United States on December 20, in conformity with the terms of the Louisiana Purchase. Details of the Louisiana Purchase are related in Chapter 11; suffice it to say here that

Spanish obstacles to the use by upriver Americans of the Mississippi and the port of New Orleans led President Thomas Jefferson to try to buy New Orleans from Napoleon, who meanwhile had induced Spain to return Louisiana to France. What began as negotiations for New Orleans ended in the acquisition of all of Louisiana, one-third of the present continental United States.

When New Orleans became American, it had a population of about eight thousand, of which half were slaves and free people of color. Although New Orleans' boom days began almost immediately, as Americans flocked into the city and its environs, it was not until the coming of the steamboat that tremendous impetus was given to New Orleans' growth and prosperity.

On January 10, 1812, Nicholas Roosevelt brought his *New Orleans*, the first steamboat on the western waters, to the levee at New Orleans, ending a voyage which had begun at Pittsburgh three and a half months earlier. There were delays en route at the Falls of the Ohio, near Louisville. When these difficulties were overcome, the *New Orleans* was further delayed by the New Madrid earthquake.

The *New Orleans* was owned by a syndicate headed by Robert R. Livingston, who, as United States minister to France, was largely responsible for the Louisiana Purchase, and Robert Fulton, whose development of the steamboat revolutionized navigation on the great rivers of America. The Livingston-Fulton group secured from the Territory of Orleans a monopoly to operate steamboats on the lower Mississippi. This monopoly was broken by Henry Shreve, who defied the authorities by sailing his *Enterprise* into the port of New Orleans late in 1814. General Andrew Jackson employed the *Enterprise* to supply Fort St. Philip, seventy-five miles below New Orleans, during the British campaign against the city. This marked the first use of a steam vessel in a military operation.

Shreve, who ultimately won out in the litigation over his successful challenge of the Livingston-Fulton monopoly, invented the snag boat to remove obstacles to navigation from the rivers. He revolutionized the design of steamboats and the engines that drove them.

In the beginning, steamboats were a curiosity, but soon they

Invented by Henry Shreve, this steam-operated snag boat removed obstructions to navigation in river channels. The Historic New Orleans Collection.

became commonplace at the New Orleans levee. In less than a decade after the *New Orleans* brought crowds to the river's edge, the *Louisiana Gazette* noted, on June 12, 1818, that "the steamboat ceased to be a novelty on the Mississippi and because of this, became a recognized agent of the commerce of the valley."

New Orleans' only significant population explosion in the 1830s was the direct result of the commerce on the river and the plantation economy that sprang up along its lush, fertile banks. In 1830 the United States census recorded New Orleans' population at 46,000; in 1840, New Orleans became the third city, after New York and Baltimore, to reach 100,000 population.

As the years passed, palatial packet steamships began to share the Mississippi with the vessels of commerce, carrying passengers

The *Natchez* and the *Robert E. Lee* competed in the 1,210-mile steamboat race in 1870 from New Orleans to St. Louis. The *Robert E. Lee* won—in 3 days, 18 hours, and 30 minutes. The Historic New Orleans Collection.

in luxury up and down the river. And showboats brought melodramas and vaudeville entertainment to the river towns and settlements clustered around the large plantations.

Because of the river, which carried the produce of the Middle West to New Orleans for export abroad, as well as the cotton and sugar from nearby plantations, New Orleans became a world port of great significance. Indeed, in 1860, on the eve of the Civil War, New Orleans was the world's greatest export center with port receipts in excess of $185 million, of which $109 million was represented by cotton for the mills of England and France.

The river had its hazards. Floods, which in ages long past had deposited rich levels of silt on the land, were a constant threat to towns and plantations, and even New Orleans itself. And steamboats were not without their dangers, too, for explosions of over-pressured boilers were far from infrequent. The greatest threat to the well-being of New Orleans that the river brought the city was that of yellow fever, which was carried into the area by ships from

The New Orleans riverfront port, shown *ca. 1850*, was crowded with commercial vessels (many carrying cotton for international export), palatial packet steamboats, and showboats. New Orleans is still one of the world's great centers of shipborne commerce. The Historic New Orleans Collection.

Latin America and the islands of the Caribbean. The carrier mosquito, the *Aedes aegypti*, swarmed in stagnant gutter water and the swamps about the city, and all that was needed to start an epidemic was a yellow fever patient aboard a ship from the tropics in the port of New Orleans. For more than one hundred years, epidemics were recurrent, as Bronze John swept up the river with an unbelievable fury.

The Mississippi River was the highroad of invasion during the Civil War. A deadly blow to the Confederacy was dealt by the Union fleet under Captain David G. Farragut, which passed the blazing fire of Forts Jackson and St. Philip and captured New Orleans in April, 1862. A little more than a year later, when Vicksburg and Port Hudson, the last Confederate bastions on the Mississippi, fell, President Lincoln was able to say: "The Father of Waters again goes unvexed to the sea."

In making its way to the sea for thousands of years, the Mississippi built most of south Louisiana by forming subdeltas through the deposit of silt. The result of all this water flowing

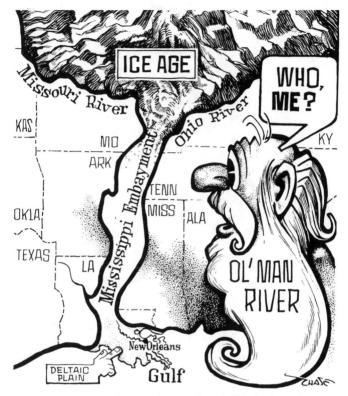

Some 20,000 years ago, after the embayment drained off the Ice Age melt waters, the sediment in the Mississippi formed the St. Francis, Yazoo, and the Tensas deltas as well as the delta land for New Orleans. Illustration by John C. Chase.

downstream was a river deep enough for navigation except at its very mouth, where silt kept building shoals. Navigators had great difficulty entering the river until after the Civil War, when Captain James Buchanan Eads devised a way to keep the river's mouth open. He did it by building jetties which use the force of the current to scour out a channel.

"Ol' Man Ribber don't say nuthin'," as the song goes, "just keeps rollin' along." Its rolling has brought to New Orleans prosperity and pestilence, trade and troubles, industry and invasion. Yet, as it

Drawing of LaSalle's ship, *La Belle,* which brought the explorer to America in search of the mouth of the Mississippi River.

was in 1718, the Mississippi River is the reason New Orleans exists. The Father of Waters is, indeed, the lifeline of a great city.

Explorer LaSalle's ship, *La Belle*, with which he led his expedition to America in the hope of colonizing Louisiana, was found in July 1995 in Matagorda Bay, Texas, buried in the sand but with its hull almost intact. The vessel had lain for more than three centuries at the bottom of the bay. It was discovered by a fisherman who hooked it when he cast a line.

LaSalle and his crew left LaRochelle, France, on August 1, 1684, in search of the mouth of the Mississippi River. Without complete navigational information, LaSalle sailed past the river's mouth by some four hundred miles. From Matagorda Bay, he and some of his men set out on foot in search of the river, which they never found. LaSalle's crew murdered the explorer as they searched in vain.

A discovery of great importance to the history of Louisiana and Texas, *LaBelle* was excavated and reassembled by archaeologists at Texas A&M University with plans to place it in the Texas History Museum at Austin.

C.L.D.

BIBLIOGRAPHY

Dufour, Charles L. *New Orleans: The Crescent City.* New York, 1967.
———. *Ten Flags in the Wind.* New York, 1967.
Read, William A. *Louisiana Place Names of Indian Origin.* University Bulletin, LSU, New Ser., XIX (February, 1927).

2.

 ## CANAL AND OTHER STREETS

There will always remain ample evidence that Canal Street in the beginning was intended to be not a street but rather a border line separating two feuding areas of New Orleans, each then called a city. One, a French city, was founded by Bienville in 1718, when the streets were planned and given the names they still bear. An American city was on the other side, but it took one hundred years and an act of Congress for it to grow and become that.

Beyond the city limits of Bienville's original settlement lay the Commons, land not part of the city and not available for private ownership either by grant or by purchase. Legally, such lands were for the common benefit of all the people, as witness the first New Orleanians who planted their vegetable gardens in the area.

At the same time New Orleans was founded, Pierre de Marigny filed for a concession on the river immediately below the town, and Bienville took possession of a similar grant on the other side. Both of these properties began beyond the city Commons. But on the lower side of town, the Commons was narrow, a scant block from the city limits, and back of the town it didn't matter. The swamp began on the other side of North Rampart Street. Only the Commons on Bienville's upper side of the city ever became important, valuable, and historically significant.

Bienville's grant was many times larger than Bienville's city, the present-day Vieux Carré. It lay along Tchoupitoulas Street—the River Road then—all the way up to Carrollton Avenue and extended back into the swamp to about Broad Street. The map also shows how the river has deposited soil and built up new land several blocks in front of Tchoupitoulas Street, actually a tract of land in itself larger than the 258.5 acres which comprise the Vieux Carré. Bienville could never have built the 1984 New Orleans fair where it was held. In 1718 that land was river bottom.

But, alas, Bienville didn't own all the present-day Central Business District and all the Uptown very long. After eight years, he sold thirty-two arpents nearest the Commons to the Jesuits for an estimated $960. The Jesuits farmed the future business district for thirty-seven years, until their order was suppressed and their properties confiscated. The Spanish Crown—by now Spain owned all Louisiana—divided the thirty-two arpents into six parcels and sold them at auction, reputedly for $180,000.

In reporting property values in Louisiana's early days, we must of necessity give valuations that are "estimated" or "reputed." Who knows the buying power of French francs or Spanish pesos then, or their percentage of exchange into U.S. dollars, money which would not appear for another hundred years.

Then there are "arpents." All properties in colonial Louisiana were measured in that ancient unit. An arpent was 192 linear feet, except when it was a square arpent. Then it was equivalent to a French acre, which was 80 percent of an English acre. Louisiana surveyors tend to become prematurely gray because old land titles do not always specify which arpent measurement is meant.

In 1788, Bertrand Gravier is identified as owner of a twelve-arpent parcel of the former Jesuit property, because he married the widow of a man who had bought it. We know it extended from Common Street to St. Joseph, because Gravier hired Carlos Trudeau to subdivide it and name the streets. Because these were Spanish times, other streets were named St. Charles for the king of Spain; Carondelet for Baron de Carondelet, the king's governor; and Baronne, for the baron's wife.

Canal Street, a boulevard with a grassy center between two 60-foot roadways, was originally planned as a canal between American and French sections. It took thirty-six years for the canal plan to be abandoned, during which time New Orleanians on both sides began calling the median strip the *neutral ground*—a term used in no other city. Illustration by John C. Chase.

These were also the years when buckskinned Kentucky and Tennessee frontiersmen began arriving on flatboats in growing numbers from the newly settled Ohio River valley, with their produce to export at the Spanish port of New Orleans. From the beginning these rough frontiersmen, who had never seen a city, and citified French and Spanish Creoles, most of whom had never seen a frontier, didn't get along. Thus was begun a longtime animosity between the two, which would influence the growth of New Orleans for many years. It actually did result in two legally organized cities of New Orleans, with Canal Street the border.

That happened March 3, 1807, just four years after the Louisiana Purchase, when the Congress of the United States made the Commons a part of New Orleans, "providing the city shall convey gratuitously for the public benefit . . . as much of [the Commons] as shall be necessary to continue the Canal of Carondelet from its present basin to the Mississippi, and shall not dispose of, for the purpose of building thereon, any lot within 60 feet of the space reserved for a canal, which shall forever remain open as a public highway." This was done. Surveyor Jacques Tanesse had completed his subdivision by 1816 which showed a canal 51 feet wide running from the turning basin of the Carondelet Canal, back of Rampart at

Canal Street, mid-1850s. The Historic New Orleans Collection.

St. Louis Street, along the rear limit of the Vieux Carré to Canal, where it continued through the Commons to the river. Also, 60-foot widths were reserved on both sides, allowing a total of 171 feet for a street that got to be called Canal. Then the streets of Bienville's original French city were continued through the Commons to Canal, where their names ended. On the other side, streets in Gravier's subdivision, which was fast becoming an American

neighborhood, also continued into the Commons with their names also ending at Canal. This should be sufficient evidence that the new wide street did not unite the two early cities of New Orleans— but there is more. When digging the canal was delayed thirty-six years before finally being abandoned, New Orleanians on both sides began calling the grassy center between the two 60-foot roadways the "neutral ground." From this beginning, as New

Orleans grew, the center of every two-lane street was called "neutral ground" all over town. The term is used in no other city.

But don't ever think the two sections were not warring communities. When the newly arrived Americans were not welcomed by the Creoles, they established themselves in the Faubourg (suburb) Ste. Marie—Gravier's new subdivision which he had thoughtfully named for his rich wife—and commenced a building program that in the end surpassed Creole efforts. The city charter of 1835 divided New Orleans into two separate cities each with its own city council, each with its own city hall. The Creoles had the Cabildo, and the Americans built their city hall (now called Gallier Hall). When the charter of 1850 united them, the American section had become and has remained the Central Business District. But nobody lost. The French Quarter—along with the river and the Louisiana Superdome—heads the city's tourist attractions.

But so much for a street named for a canal it never had. By the time of the Civil War it had become New Orleans' most famous street. Now it begins at the river and ends at the cemeteries, or begins in the cemeteries and ends in the river. (New Orleanians are still debating that.) Also, Canal Street has become a point of orientation. All street numbers begin at Canal, and the names of all streets that cross it are "South" on the uptown side, and "North" on the downtown side. This in spite of the fact that South Claiborne runs northwest and North Claiborne runs southeast. In New Orleans the compass is something else again. On the lakefront, for instance, East End is west of West End. Directions are given as uptown, downtown, riverside, lakeside, mid-city, and lakefront.

When there were many streetcar lines all but one ran to Canal Street and before that all the horsecars did. Canal was considered by experienced women shoppers the only place worth their time. At Carnival all the parades went to Canal Street, and pictures captioned "Mardi Gras on Canal Street" were always page-one copy in Ash Wednesday editions. It's clear from such mob scene pictures that all the people went to Canal Street at Mardi Gras time.

But, alas, one of the "widest streets in the world" is no longer wide enough to accommodate the increased population since

Canal Street today, from the top of the International Trade Mart. Photo by
A. J. Meek.

World War II. Now all the famous Canal Street stores have branches in more than one of the suburban shopping centers. As for Carnival parades—which have doubled and redoubled in number—many organizations have found attendance at parades in their own neighborhoods sufficiently rewarding.

Seemingly, however, the more Canal Street changes the more it remains the same. It began as a street of fine homes, of which the Boston Club is the only remaining example. Judah Touro led the way in making it a shopping center. He built a block-long building for shops and even made the street an heir in his will, leaving $150,000 for its beautification. In 1855, the city council changed Canal's name to Touro. But nobody called it that, and the name was changed back to Canal.

Since the 1970s more and more tall hotels are springing up on the famous old street. Canal may not revert to an antebellum neighborhood of homes, but so many new hotels certainly are providing homes away from home for a growing number of New Orleans visitors here to see the French Quarter, the river, and the Superdome. Well, all three can be seen from hotel windows on Canal Street.

J.C.C.

3.

⚜ THE VIEUX CARRÉ ⚜

The Vieux Carré is the original New Orleans, laid out in 1721 on orders of Jean-Baptiste Le Moyne, Sieur de Bienville, founder of the city. Vieux Carré, pronounced approximately "v-yer ka-ray," means Old Square, but it really isn't a square at all. It is a rectangle, bounded by the Mississippi River, Iberville Street, Esplanade Avenue, and Rampart Street. The last was named for the ramparts that once afforded only token protection to the city from attack on its rear.

The popular name for the Vieux Carré is the French Quarter, although, oddly enough, there is only one authentic French building within its limits. This is the old Ursuline Convent, 1114 Chartres Street, which dates from 1750 and is generally considered to be the oldest structure in the Mississippi Valley.

Why is there only one French building in the French Quarter? Because two devastating fires, during the last years of the Spanish regime, swept away all other French buildings. The first fire, in 1788, destroyed 856 buildings, with a loss of more than $2 million, a staggering amount in those days. What the first fire left standing, the second fire in 1794 wiped out. Accordingly, the French Quarter, as visited by hundreds of thousands of people each year, was built by the Spaniards and Americans who flocked to New Orleans after the Louisiana Purchase.

So only the Ursuline Convent, a splendid example of French Colonial architecture in America, survived the two fires. It is

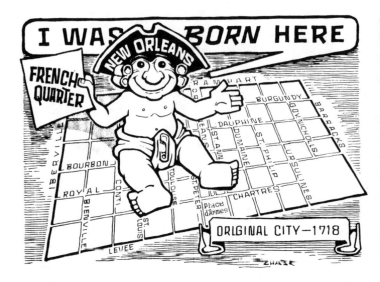

Map by John C. Chase

sometimes claimed for the building known as Madame John's Legacy (632 Dumaine Street) that it too withstood the flames of both fires, but responsible architectural historians discount this claim. This is not to say, however, that Madame John's Legacy is not an important old building in the Vieux Carré.

The Vieux Carré, which the French engineer Adrien de Pauger began laying out in 1721, is today one of America's outstanding tourist attractions. Timber houses were almost universal before the fires of 1788 and 1794, but the Spanish authorities, after the second conflagration, passed rigid building laws requiring all two-story houses to be built of brick or of timber frames filled with brick between the upright posts. The timber had to be covered with cement at least one inch thick, and the buildings were to have flat roofs covered with tile and brick.

Although the Vieux Carré today dates, except for the Ursuline Convent, from Spanish and American days, the French influence still prevailed, as a distinguished architectural historian, Samuel Wilson, Jr., has pointed out in his authoritative monograph on the French Quarter: "The Vieux Carré, in its architectural character today, is the result of two and a half centuries of growth, reflecting the influence of changing times and diverse nationalities. While little remains of the buildings of the French colonial period, the influence of the French cultural background of much of the population continued to be felt in building style and technique well into the nineteenth century. Much that the early French developed was carried on, adopted or modified by subsequent Spanish and American settlers."

The exploitation of Louisiana was originally assigned to the wealthy merchant Antoine Crozat, who in 1712 was given a charter with the exclusive right to trade in Louisiana for fifteen years. This proved a losing proposition and Crozat, after five years, asked the Crown to release him from the charter. Louis XIV, having died in 1715, was succeeded by his great-grandson Louis XV, a child of only five years of age. The regent, Philippe d'Orléans, did not have to look far for someone to take up the discarded Louisiana charter. His friend, John Law, the amazing Scotsman whose financial wizardry ultimately lost its magic, had organized a private bank which was highly successful. He now proposed to organize a company to exploit Louisiana. On September 6, 1717, Law's Company of the West was chartered for twenty-five years.

One of the Company of the West's first actions was the decision to establish a town on the Mississippi River and name it for the regent. An undated, but unquestionably in September, 1717, resolution by the company reads: "Resolved that they will establish, thirty leagues up the river, a town which they will name New Orleans, which one may reach by the river and by Lake Pontchartrain."

Just when Bienville, in 1718, first began to clear the site for New Orleans is not known with certainty, but in a report to the Ministry of the Marine on June 12, Bienville wrote: "We are working at present on the establishment of New Orleans, thirty leagues above the entrance to the Mississippi." In 1968, when New

Orleans celebrated the 250th anniversary of its founding, the city fathers designated April 16 as the official date when work began.

Plans for the layout of New Orleans were drawn by Le Blond de la Tour, chief engineer in Louisiana; his assistant, Adrien de Pauger, began surveying the site of what is now the Vieux Carré on March 29, 1721.

The heart of the Vieux Carré is Jackson Square, which Pauger laid out as the parade ground or Place d'Armes. It was also such under the Spanish, with the appropriate change of name to Plaza de Armas. It became the Public Square when the Americans took over Louisiana. It was not until 1851 that it was named Jackson Square, in honor of the hero of the Battle of New Orleans, General Andrew Jackson.

Jackson Square is unique among America's most impressive architectural assemblies, flanked as it is by the St. Louis Cathedral (1851), Cabildo (1795), and Presbytère (1795), facing the river, and the twin Pontalba Buildings (1850) on the two other sides. Moreover, Jackson Square is one of the nation's most historical spots. During colonial days, French and Spanish troops paraded here, and edicts of government were promulgated. It was here that Alexander O'Reilly landed his Spanish troops when he came to suppress the bloodless revolution of 1768.

It was here in 1803 that the flag of Bourbon Spain gave way to the Tricolor of the French Republic on November 30; twenty days later the French flag came down and the American flag was hoisted. It was here, too, that Jackson was triumphantly received after his victory over the British at Chalmette in 1815. Other notable celebrations here were for the Marquis de Lafayette in 1825; for Jackson's return in 1840 to lay the cornerstone for the pedestal of a future monument; for General Zachary Taylor in 1847; for President Charles de Gaulle of France in 1960. President Dwight D. Eisenhower attended the reenactment of the Louisiana Purchase transfer in Jackson Square in 1953. During the observance of the 150th anniversary of the Battle of New Orleans in 1965, many events were held in Jackson Square.

The equestrian statue of General Jackson, by the American

St. Louis Cathedral, flanked by the Cabildo and the Presbytère, was completed in 1851, succeeding two earlier churches, one of which was destroyed by fire. These structures face Jackson Square (formerly the Place d'Armes) and, across Decatur Street, the levee. Photo by A. J. Meek.

At Café du Monde, in the Vieux Carré near the levee, tourists and city dwellers alike enjoy coffee and beignets, a traditional New Orleans breakfast and brunch treat. Photo by A. J. Meek.

sculptor Clark Mills, was dedicated on February 9, 1856, with the sculptor, himself, one of the speakers. The ten-ton statue, according to a contemporary account, employed "a new principle, which was to have the hind legs of the horse exactly under the center of the body, which, of course, produced a perfect balance, thereby giving the horse more the appearance of life."

The importance of Clark Mills's statue—there are replicas in Washington, across from the White House, and at the Tennessee state capitol in Nashville—has been noted by Lorado Taft, distinguished critic: "He [Mills] never had seen an equestrian statue; there was none in this country to see. It seems at first strange that America's initial performance in this line should be an attempt of surpassing audacity, but it is the story of all beginnings. . . . At any rate, he built a colossal horse, adroitly balanced on its hind legs, and America gazed with bated breath. Nobody knows or cares whether the rider looks like Jackson or not; the extraordinary pose of the horse absorbs all attention, all admiration."

Houses in the Vieux Carré were constructed flush with the sidewalks. The inner courts, or patios, with shrubs and flowers, were thus hidden from the street. Another distinctive feature of the houses in the French Quarter is the ornamental ironwork—some wrought iron and some cast iron—that adorns the balconies. Of this Mark Twain wrote: "The pattern of the wrought iron railing is often exceedingly light and dainty, and airy and graceful . . . a delicate web of baffling, intricate forms." And of the buildings that have these lovely displays of "iron lace," Twain declared: "The houses are massed in blocks; are austerely plain and dignified; uniform of pattern, with here and there a departure from it with pleasing effect. . . . Their chief beauty is the deep, warm, varicolored stain, with which time and the weather have enriched the plaster. It harmonizes with all the surroundings, and has a natural look of belonging there as has the flush upon sunset clouds. This charming decoration cannot be successfully imitated; neither is it to be found elsewhere in America."

As long as a century ago the Vieux Carré went into decline. The critic, Charles Dudley Warner, summed it up in 1887: "The

Farmers' Market in the French Quarter. Photo by A. J. Meek.

French Quarter is out of repair . . . it is a city of the past, specially interesting in its picturesque decay." Slowly but steadily the Vieux Carré slipped into a slum area by the end of World War I. And then in the early 1920s, the renaissance of the French Quarter began. Old houses, worth a fortune today, were picked up for a song by newcomers to the city as well as by farsighted New Orleanians, and rehabilitation of the Vieux Carré was under way. By both state law and city ordinance, the Vieux Carré Commission, created by the legislature in 1936, is charged with preserving the "quaint and distinctive character" of the French Quarter.

In contrast to the old-world charm which pervades most of the Vieux Carré, there is Bourbon Street with its tinseled tawdriness. It is the "strippers' strip," rowdy and raucous, and filled with people from before dusk to long after midnight every day.

A visitor to New Orleans can enjoy a stroll through the Vieux Carré, merely window-shopping antiques, poking into picturesque patios, or mingling with the crowd in Jackson Square.

C.L.D.

BIBLIOGRAPHY

Chase, John C. *Frenchmen, Desire, Good Children and Other Streets of New Orleans*. 3rd ed. New York, 1979.

Dufour, Charles L., and Bernard Hermann. *New Orleans*. New Orleans, 1980.

Wilson, Samuel, Jr. *A Guide to Architecture of New Orleans, 1699–1959*. New York, 1959.

4.

 THE GARDEN DISTRICT

New Orleans' Garden District was once the city of Lafayette. It grew into an area of handsome antebellum homes in the Greek Revival style in the golden age when men made fortunes in the cotton, sugar, and coffee trade.

These homes, which feature Ionic, Doric, or Corinthian columns and beautiful cast-iron lacework framing spacious porches and balconies, still stand today. They house many of the city's wealthier families now, as they did in the two decades prior to the Civil War when many of them were built. They equal in elegance those found in many cities throughout the South. And, they are located in an area measuring roughly twelve by five blocks, from St. Charles Avenue to Magazine Street, and Jackson Avenue to Louisiana Avenue. The fact that they were built within two miles of what was to become the Central Business District of a major metropolitan city, and have continued to be occupied and kept in their original state, makes them a unique collection of mansions.

Wealth and a desire to live in a style of elegance led to the development of the Garden District. Following the Louisiana Purchase in 1803, New Orleans slowly began to find itself in the world of commerce. The riverfront began to teem with activity, goods moving down the Mississippi River from the Midwest and the East, to be loaded onto ships bound for Europe or the Atlantic Coast of the United States. Agriculture in the South began to

The graceful iron fence and the gallery decoration at 1315 First Street are fine examples of the distinctive New Orleans ironwork. Photo by A. J. Meek.

Map by John C. Chase

prosper. New Orleans became, for the Mississippi Valley, the natural port for shipment of cotton, sugar, lumber, and other commodities. Conversely, it became a port of entry for such commodities as coffee and European manufactured goods.

This torrent of trade established on the Mississippi and fed outward to the world began to build millionaires as well as the Queen City of the South. By 1850, New Orleans had a population of some 116,000 and was the wealthiest city in the South. The merchants and professional men began to look for places to build homes that would reflect their status in life. The Vieux Carré, the city's original settlement, was already crowded. The newly prosperous merchants, mostly Americans, turned to the city of Lafayette for spacious grounds on which to build their sumptuous mansions.

Local historians say the area came by its name naturally. There are two versions, each plausible, and both probably correct. Until the advent of the Garden District, New Orleanians had lived in houses walled off from the street, with balconies overlooking small interior courtyards. In the new section, houses were being built on large lots which permitted gardens for beautification.

These gardens grew, another story goes, because a crevasse on the Macarty plantation several miles upstream from the Garden District caused the ensuing flood to deposit a fertile layer of silt over what became the Garden District. That layer of silt resulted in lush growth, in New Orleans' semitropical climate.

The origin of the Garden District can be traced back to the time when Jacques François Esnould Dugué de Livaudais established a plantation just above New Orleans. Its lower boundaries began at what today is Felicity Street, running to above Ninth Street (now Harmony) and stretching from the river to LaSalle Street (formerly St. George). This was the Faubourg Livaudais. (Faubourg: outside the city, suburb.)

Livaudais had married Celeste de Marigny, daughter of a large property-holder said to have been the wealthiest man in Louisiana at the time. In 1825, Madame Livaudais separated from Livaudais and moved to Paris. In the separation settlement, Livaudais granted her title to the plantation. She sold it for $490,000 to a group of real estate promoters who in turn cut it up into a residential district. Benjamin Buisson, who had been an engineer in Napoleon's army, was hired to lay out the area's streets and lots. All the property was placed on the market, except the grounds where Madame Livaudais' house was being built. The home never was completed, falling into ruins and finally burning during the Civil War.

The Faubourg Livaudais became the major part of the city of Lafayette. In the early 1840s, when many of the Garden District homes were rising, Lafayette had a population of 12,651 plus 1,539 slaves. Horses, mules, and goats ran loose in the streets. Lafayette, incorporated in 1833, was named in honor of the French nobleman who had fought with Washington in the Revolution and who had recently visited New Orleans. It was annexed by New Orleans in 1852.

The area held a double attraction for prospective homebuilders; it was near New Orleans and the river—easily accessible by horse-drawn vehicles. A horse-drawn omnibus ran from Canal Street to Lafayette. A mule-drawn branch railroad also served the area. Steamboats unloaded their cargoes on the levee just a few blocks away, while ocean-going ships discharged their goods downstream. Negro slaves, readily abundant, made it possible for wealthy people to maintain their lavish homes.

The oldest house still standing in the Garden District is believed to have been built in 1838 by Thomas Toby at 2340 Prytania Street. The son of a Philadelphia marine insurance agent, Toby had prospered in New Orleans as a wheelwright and commission merchant. Although New Orleans was a center of trade for lumber, his house was built largely of lumber brought from Pennsylvania. Toby, a victim of one of the era's financial collapses, lost his fortune. His house was sold at auction following his death in 1849. His lot befell many other financial titans of the day who had built the homes, but the mansions have endured through the years, most of them as beautiful now as the day they were opened.

Mark Twain wrote after a visit to the Garden District: "All of the dwellings . . . have a comfortable look. Those in the wealthy quarter are spacious, painted snowy white, usually, and generally have wide verandas, or double verandas, supported by ornamental columns. These mansions stand in the center of large grounds and rise, garlanded with roses, out of the midst of swelling masses of shining green foliage and many-colored blossoms. No houses could be in better harmony with their surroundings, or more pleasing to the eye, or more homelike and comfortable looking." (Thus did Twain support one version of how the area got its name.)

Twain often visited George Washington Cable, internationally known for his Creole stories and songs, at Cable's residence at 1313 Eighth Street, between Chestnut and Coliseum. On one occasion they met in lively discussion with other noted literary persons of the era—Charles Dudley Warner of *Harper's Magazine*, Lafcadio Hearn, and Joel Chandler Harris.

The fame of the district extends beyond its architectural and

Believed to have been built in about 1860, this cottage at 2423 Prytania Street has an unusual curved side gallery. Photo by A. J. Meek.

literary excellence, however. It is the site of the old Southern Athletic Club, later Behrman Gymnasium, where Jake Kilrain trained for his fight with John L. Sullivan in 1889 at Richburg, Mississippi. The gym was situated on Washington Avenue, corner of Prytania. Here, too, "Gentleman Jim" Corbett trained for his fight with Sullivan at the old Olympic Club in New Orleans.

Most of the area's historical fame parallels the antebellum and Civil War era. General Benjamin ("Spoons") Butler, the scourge of New Orleans who took command of the city after it fell to Union forces, was rebuffed when he tried to take over one Garden District home for his own. Butler had confiscated a home at 1420 Euterpe, in the Lower Garden District, for use as a Freedmen's Bureau. He then wanted personally to occupy the home built by James Robb on Washington Avenue, between Camp and Chestnut. This mansion was occupied by John Burnside, a wealthy planter. The story goes that Butler appeared at the door to press his demand, but the canny Burnside protested that he was a British citizen, and thus out of the general's jurisdiction. He got away with it. Butler, instead, took over the home of Confederate General David E. Twiggs at 1115 Prytania, near Calliope. The Robb home was demolished after serving as Newcomb College and later as the Southern Baptist Bible Institute.

Jefferson Davis, president of the Confederacy, died in the home at 1134 First Street. It is a house with broad galleries and Ionic and Corinthian columns, typically Garden District, and the one in which Davis' daughter Winnie had made her debut. Davis had arrived in New Orleans gravely ill, unable to continue the journey to his Gulf Coast home at Beauvoir. Dr. Jacob Upshaw Payne, a friend, took him to his First Street home, where Davis died on December 6, 1889.

Beneath the gables and behind the graceful iron fences of most of the Garden District homes lie stories of interest. The architecture of the homes stands out as some of the most splendorous of the nineteenth century, not only in the South but within the United States. While many of the homes predate the Civil War, there was considerable construction following the war, extending even into the early twentieth century.

With broad galleries and Ionic and Corinthian columns typical of Garden District architecture, this house was once the Payne residence. It was here at 1134 First Street that Jefferson Davis, president of the Confederacy, died on December 6, 1889. Photo by A. J. Meek.

It's easy to see the Garden District. Here's how:

Take a streetcar, or go by automobile. If you are a guest at one of the Vieux Carré or Central Business District (Canal Street area) hotels, you will find it convenient to board a streetcar at St. Charles and Common streets and ride to Jackson Avenue, or above, depending on where you wish to start. (See map on page 50.) You may then take a leisurely walk up and down the principal streets of the district, and get a closeup view of most of the homes within an hour or two. Naturally, driving would reduce the time. Riding the streetcar is not only convenient but fun, and there are restaurants in the Washington Avenue area in which to dine following the tour.

There are dozens of magnificent homes in the Garden District. A list of some of the most historic and famous landmarks follows.

On Prytania Street

2127   A Greek Revival–style mansion built in 1857–1858 with front and side balconies featuring Corinthian columns and cast-iron grillwork. An outstanding example of Louisiana plantation architecture.

2221   Built in 1850 when the area was part of the city of Lafayette, this is considered one of the best works of noted architect Henry Howard. Italian villa with majestic columns.

2340   Believed to have been built about 1838, this raised cottage is set on brick piers, with ground-level basement. It was built for Thomas Toby, who came to New Orleans from Philadelphia. Marble mantels and fireplaces are found in almost every room. The handmade window panes glisten brightly.

2343   A Renaissance-style mansion designed by architect James Freret, it was built in 1872 during the second period of affluence in the Garden District. The home was constructed for Bradish Johnson, who made a fortune in sugar plantations, but since 1929 has been used to house the Louise S. McGehee School. Its winding staircase, high ceilings, and unusual molding establish it as a masterpiece of design. Notice the beautiful Corinthian columns and the classic design of the windows.

2423   Believed to have been built at the start of the Civil War, this cottage features an unusual curved side gallery.

2507   Built in 1852, this is a classic of the antebellum era. Ionic and Corinthian columns support broad galleries set off with the traditional iron grillwork found in New Orleans. Most rooms

A stunning example of the architecture to be found in the Garden District is 2504 Prytania Street. Photo by A. J. Meek.

Cornstalk fence, 1448 Fourth Street. Photo by A. J. Meek.

measure twenty-two feet square, with a ballroom twenty-two by forty-four feet. Ceilings of hand-painted pictures and Italian marble mantels give it a touch of elegance.

2520   Constructed in 1853, this mansion is noted for its gallery supported by cast-iron columns, which set the house apart from others in the area.

2521   Built in 1857, this once lavish home has for many years served as the Mother of Perpetual Help chapel. Its marble entrance hall and finely detailed cast-iron work on the galleries are works of distinction.

2605   A Gothic-style cottage believed to have been built in 1849, this house contrasts sharply with its neighbors. Walks, lawn, and shrubbery give it a real Garden District touch.

On Fourth Street

1448   A New Orleans version of the Italian villa, this house was built in 1859 for a Kentucky colonel for less than $25,000. The cast-iron fence, in cornstalk pattern, is a talk piece of the area. Ornamental ironwork on the columns, and framing the galleries, makes it outstanding.

1538   The two-story mansion was built in 1864 and features galleries embellished with heavy cast-iron grillwork.

On Third Street

1213   Built about 1867. Notice the broad overhanging roofs and the spectacular galleries. This home is said to be an outstanding example of post–Civil War construction. Dense shrubbery and trees make it necessary to view the house at close range.

1331   A classic example of the Italian villa, this house was built by the famous New Orleans architect James Gallier, Sr., about 1850 for a prominent merchant. Its cast-iron galleries are regarded as the most picturesque in the area. Heart pine floors and free-standing stairs are special features.

1415   Another example of the Italian villa. Built in the late 1850s, this house has two stories of equal height, fifteen feet eight inches. The rounded galleries with both Doric and Corinthian columns give it a different look. The living and dining rooms have artistically painted ceilings, delicately patterned medallions, and a striking crystal chandelier.

On Philip Street

1220   Built in the late 1850s, this mansion has fluted Corinthian columns on the lower and upper stories, along with the traditional grillwork. A semi-octagonal bay on the north side gives it a special dimension. Following the Civil War, Isaac Delgado, whose bequest founded the New Orleans Museum of Art, resided here with an aunt and uncle. He began his art collection here.

1238   A Greek Revival structure, built in 1853–1854, this home is set off with octagonal bays on one side. The walls are eighteen inches thick, and the ceilings rise to fourteen feet, as do many others throughout the area.

On First Street

1134   Jefferson Davis, president of the Confederacy, died here on December 6, 1889. The home was built in 1849–1850 and is considered a masterpiece of the Greek Revival architecture seen on plantations throughout the South. It has walls of stuccoed brick, cypress beams, heart pine floors, and window and door frames of mahogany. A lavish garden adds the final touch.

1239   Built in 1857 for $13,000, this house has Corinthian and Ionic columns in the center and plain pilasters on each end of the porch. The rose-design grillwork embellishes its galleries handsomely. A sideyard garden provides a natural setting.

1331   A profusion of cast-iron grillwork makes this house a photographer's dream. A spectacular sight.

On Coliseum Street

2627   This Swiss chalet type has intricate jigsaw scrollwork in its gables. Elaborately decorated galleries with cast-iron grillwork show the New Orleans influence.

2618   Built in the 1840s, this is considered a good example of the Greek Revival–style house with portico.

On Jackson Avenue

1224   This Civil War–era raised cottage has a semi-octagonal bay on one side.

1410   Built about 1856 as a home, it has housed the Soule Business College in more recent years. It has the traditional Greek columns and balconies and is a landmark of the avenue. The grillwork is considered exceptional, as is the iron fence.

On Washington Avenue

1126   Fluted columns support a graceful gallery which juts outward. Tastefully decorated with grillwork.

On Eighth Street

1313   The raised plantation-type cottage was George Washington Cable's home and the scene of gatherings of the literary figures of the era. Simple wooden columns and arched column supports reflect the southern home atmosphere.

W.G.C.

BIBLIOGRAPHY

Roehl, Marjorie. "The People of the Garden District." New Orleans *States-Item*, March 7–11, 14–18, 1977.

Samuel, Martha, and Ray Samuel. *The Great Days of the Garden District and the Old City of Lafayette*. New Orleans, 1961.

Wilson, Samuel, Jr. *A Guide to Architecture of New Orleans, 1699–1959*. New York, 1959.

5.

❦ THE CEMETERIES ❦

New Orleans lays its dead to rest both underground and above-ground, in plain graves marked by simple headstones and in elaborate tombs and vaults of marble and granite embellished by monuments which are imposing as well as historic. They were also a necessity, because of the extremely high water table. Its cemeteries reflect the growth of the city and the pain it has endured through epidemics, floods, fires, and wars. Handsome tombs and monuments pay tribute to the great and the not-so-great—to the heroes of the Battle of New Orleans, the Civil War, World Wars I and II, and the lesser conflicts. They also memorialize gamblers, governors, mayors, the son of a president of the United States, kings and queens of Carnival, a voodoo queen, and even a noted madam of the city's once notorious red-light district, Storyville.

In displaying bereavement, and recognition, for its fallen sons and daughters through the years, this Creole city created not only some of the most unusual cemeteries in America but a major tourist attraction as well. The old cemeteries, with their wrought-iron gates and fanciful religious decorations, tastefully sculptured statues of stone and simple graves bearing unusual inscriptions, stand high on the list of things visitors want to see. Tour buses daily transport hundreds to some of the most distinctive cemeteries in the United States. The kinds of ornamental ironwork found on many of New Orleans' old buildings and residences are also seen in most of its cemeteries.

Beautiful gates and fences of wrought and cast iron enclose architecturally designed tombs that reflect the style of life, and the times, of the deceased. A walk through any one of several of the historic burial grounds will give the visitor a view of a variety of skillful designs which decorate the tombs, vaults, and graves— and a sense of history.

The patterns of design of the ironwork coincide with styles popular during the various periods of the city's history. There are spearlike picket fences, graceful arches, crosses indicating a person's ancestry, insets with floral and musical motifs, religious symbols and simple geometrical figures, most with artistic touches. In 1845, tombs costing as much as $30,000 were being built; in recent years the most elaborate tombs cost many times that amount. Families built expensive tombs or monuments to give tangible testimony to their reverence for their dead. Wealth was not always a factor.

Tombs with distinctive iron fences in St. Louis Cemetery, No. 1. Photo by A. J. Meek.

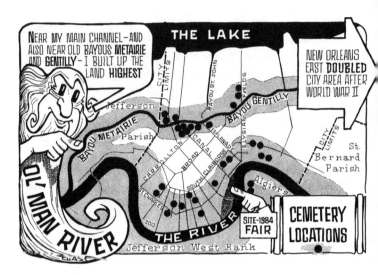

Map by John C. Chase

The cemeteries are as picturesque as they are historic. Tombs and mausoleums built to resemble Greek and Roman temples, Egyptian pyramids, and French and English structures may be seen in great numbers. Classical Revival architecture predominates in some of the older cemeteries. Tombs of brick made by slaves in New Orleans are common in the oldest graveyard, St. Louis No. 1, where the stepped-top tomb predominates. The sarcophagus form, often decorated with torches or crosses, is common in some of the cemeteries. The pedimented sarcophagus style became popular in the nineteenth century, its decorative carvings and other ornamentations said to have been the result of the influence of those in cemeteries in Paris and Rome. The frequent use of ironwork is a distinguishing mark of New Orleans funerary architecture. There are some thirty cemeteries in New Orleans, and ironwork is found in most of them.

New Orleans honors its dead each year on All Saints' Day, November 1, with displays of flowers which transform the cemeteries into virtual gardens. A religious holiday of the Catholic church, All Saints' is a day of special prayer and remembrance for the dead. In tribute to their loved ones, New Orleanians flock to the graves and tombs to place bouquets of chrysanthemums and other floral decorations. Florists report their biggest sales of the year for that day.

In no other part of the United States, according to one historian, is the practice of entombment so prevalent as it is in New Orleans, beginning with St. Louis No. 1. This practice is believed to have been brought from Spain, where wall vaults and large tombs had been in use for centuries. And, like some of those European cemeteries, the early cemeteries in New Orleans were walled. Walls enclose St. Louis Nos. 1 and 2, the earliest of the city's cemeteries. Those, and some of the more recent, have been described as cities of the dead because of the manner in which they were laid out with broad avenues and streets, many wide enough for vehicular traffic.

While the cemeteries are spread over a large area, thirteen are nestled in the area where Canal Street terminates, near Metairie Road and City Park Avenue. This group contains some of the most picturesque tombs. For years, you could ride on streetcars marked CEMETERIES, and they took you to the cluster. When buses supplanted streetcars on that route some years back, the designation was dropped, however.

Not only can you see many of the cemeteries in this cluster from present-day buses, but motorists traveling to and from the city on the Pontchartrain Expressway get a full view of rows of glistening white tombs. Because of the practice of building such large tombs and monuments, New Orleans' cemeteries are visible from many streets. The fact that the tombs are placed on small lots creates a compactness that increases visibility. New Orleans, a land-poor city built on swampy terrain, could never afford the luxury of wide, or large, lots for residences or burial plots. Drainage problems always have necessitated maximum use of land.

Unwanted water plagued the lives of early New Orleanians, and continued to inconvenience them after death. Some of the 50,000 acres of the central city—the part the map shows—are four feet below sea level. Prior to the twentieth century a grave dug the classic six-foot depth quickly filled up with four feet of water, so high was the area's water table.

A few years into the 1900s, newly installed drainage pipes of the Sewerage and Water Board, created by the 1899 Louisiana Legislature, began to dry out the soil and interment below ground became possible. However, the style—indeed, the architecture—of New Orleans cemeteries had become monumental tombs for final resting places of loved ones. Tombs still characterize New Orleans cemeteries, and probably always will.

The map is self-explanatory, and the delta land the river builds up is always highest adjacent to the channels of flowing water made brown by the millions of tons of Mississippi River valley topsoil. Of necessity all of the three-score city cemeteries in the map are shown located on the higher ground. (The following descriptions of the major cemeteries are based on the published works of Leonard V. Huber, Peggy McDowell, Mary Louise Christovich, Samuel Wilson, Jr., and Henri A. Gandolfo.)

St. Louis No. 1

Established in 1789, and the oldest current cemetery, this is the cemetery of the colonial period, with rows of boxlike tombs. New Orleans' first cemetery was opened in 1725, seven years after the city was founded, on the site of what is now the upper side of St. Peter Street, between Burgundy and Rampart. This burial ground lasted for seventy years, during which time Louisiana passed from France to Spain (1762) and grew from a village to a small town. Burials here were underground. The water level was so high that river sand had to be carted to the cemetery to build levees around the areas containing graves, and coffins had to be weighted to keep them from floating.

In 1788 New Orleans was hit by a series of disasters. A fire wiped out 856 buildings, the river overflowed, and an epidemic of what may have been yellow fever killed hundreds. Thus, the city fathers hastened to open St. Louis No. 1 on the edge of the city, at a site now located between Basin, Conti, Treme, and St. Louis streets.

The custom of aboveground burial creates some remarkably picturesque views, as here in Greenwood Cemetery. Photo by A. J. Meek.

St. Louis No. 1 contains the remains of dueling victims; sailors from ships from England, France, and Spain; the first mayor of New Orleans; Etienne Boré, the father of the Louisiana sugar industry; a world chess champion, Paul Morphy; a former governor, Pierre Derbigny; voodoo queen Marie Laveau; and many other notables. This was the original burial place of the first American governor of Louisiana, William Charles Coles Claiborne, whose remains later were moved to Metairie Cemetery. Two men killed in the Battle of New Orleans are buried here.

The custom of one vault for multiple burials was put into use here. The receptacles resemble bakers' ovens, and the vaults rise five, six, and seven crypts high, a practical way to conserve space and avoid some of the drainage problems as well. Many of these vaults today are in ruins. Interestingly, today's mausoleums follow the practice of multiple vault burials.

New Orleans was almost totally Catholic when St. Louis No. 1 was established. Protestants and Negroes were interred in the rear of that cemetery, in a swamplike area. In 1822, Girod Cemetery, built by Christ Church, became the prime Protestant burial ground. It ceased to exist in 1957, and today the Louisiana Superdome sits on part of the site. When the last remains were being moved, a number of cast-iron coffins resembling those of ancient Egypt were unearthed. They were body-shaped with a pane of glass on the front near the top.

St. Louis No. 2

This cemetery came into being in 1823. It is bounded by Iberville, Bienville, Conti, and St. Louis streets, bordering North Claiborne Avenue. Like No. 1, No. 2 is a collection of quaint tombs and vaults, many now dilapidated. The vaults are contained in walls around the cemetery, and the tombs are placed irregularly, showing little planning. This is thought to have resulted from hasty burials during epidemics. Stepped-top tombs are found in abundance in Nos. 1 and 2. They are constructed of slave brick, marble, or granite, many of them tall and narrow with vertical chambers. Facades of some have carvings and other ornamentations typical of tombs in European cemeteries. The use of ornamental iron came into widespread use here and developed into a theme for embellishment of tombs in other local cemeteries. The ironwork added an architectural dimension indigenous to New Orleans.

St. Louis No. 2 is the resting place of impresario John Davis (1773–1839); three early mayors, James Pitot, Nicholas Girod, who served in 1814–1815, and Charles Genois, who served in 1838; and a black lieutenant governor of the Reconstruction era, Oscar J. Dunn. The tomb which attracts perhaps the most attention is that of Dominique You. He was a pirate captain and smuggler and expert artillerist who catapulted to fame when given command of a battery by General Andrew Jackson during the Battle of New Orleans, January 8, 1815. You was a member of the band of pirates headed by the flamboyant Jean Laffite, who went to Jackson's aid against the British. He was the subject of a movie, *The Buccaneer*, produced in 1938 and premiered in New Orleans with Cecil B. De Mille, the producer, in attendance.

St. Louis No. 3

More epidemics, principally of yellow fever, led to the need for St. Louis No. 3. These epidemics occurred in the 1830s and the 1840s, but St. Louis No. 3 was not consecrated until 1854 following a massive yellow fever epidemic. Meantime, an area along Orleans Avenue from Broad to Bayou St. John was used. St. Louis No. 3 is situated on Esplanade Avenue near Bayou St. John. You enter through elaborate cast-iron gates topped by a graceful arch with filigree, on which sits a white cross. This cemetery, in better condition than the other St. Louis cemeteries, is the burial ground for many prominent New Orleanians. Spreading over several blocks, its tombs rise to ten feet or more, and its broad, straight streets give it the appearance of a small city of marble and granite structures.

Walled vaults in St. Louis Cemetery, No. 1. Photo by A. J. Meek.

Metairie

Metairie, showplace of all New Orleans cemeteries, is the largest in the area, spreading over 150 acres and containing more than 7,000 tombs and plots. It is a landscaped garden of tombs beautified by lagoons, stone bridges, palms, live oaks, flowers, and shrubs.

Metairie Cemetery is located at Metairie Road and Pontchartrain Boulevard. It is built on the site of the Metairie Race Course, which flourished in the mid-1850s. Legend, for which there is no factual evidence, states that the racetrack was doomed when it refused to admit lottery operator Charles T. Howard to its exclusive Jockey Club. Howard vowed, the legend holds, that he would buy the track and turn it into a cemetery. However, history records that the track experienced financial difficulty before it was sold to Howard. In 1861 the Metairie Course was used briefly as a staging area for Louisiana Confederate troops.

The Metairie Cemetery Association was chartered in May of 1872. The configuration of the track led to easy mapping of the cemetery. The track, incidentally, once was the site of encampments of the Colapissa Indians, who hunted, fished, and tilled the soil along the banks of Metairie Bayou, long since filled in. (The name Metairie, meaning "small farms," was given the area by the French.)

Metairie's monuments, tombs, and vaults are the most imposing to be found in New Orleans' cemeteries. For instance, a sixty-foot-high shaft topped by a cross rises on a plot eighty-five feet in diameter, tribute of Dan Moriarity to his wife. Four statues, representing Faith, Hope, Charity, and Memory, adorn the granite grave.

One of the most striking monuments is the equestrian statue of Confederate General Albert Sidney Johnston, which sits atop the tomb of the Army of Tennessee. For four years the tomb of the Army of Northern Virginia held the remains of Jefferson Davis, president of the Confederate States of America, who died in New Orleans on December 6, 1889. Davis was interred in Metairie following the largest funeral ever held in New Orleans. A statue of Stonewall Jackson is a feature of the Army of Northern Virginia tomb.

Davis died in a home at First and Camp streets, in the fashionable Garden District, after becoming ill aboard a steamboat while on a trip up the Mississippi River. Brought to New Orleans, he was too ill to be taken to his home at Beauvoir on the Mississippi Gulf Coast, and so was taken to the home of a friend.

His family and friends planned to bury him after a simple ceremony at Beauvoir, but when they began to receive hundreds of telegrams from persons wishing to attend the funeral this plan was abandoned. Southern governors vied for the honor of burying him in their own states. Confederate veterans' associations, generals, senators, and hundreds of leading citizens throughout the South wired that they desired to attend. This posed a dilemma for Mrs. Davis. The mayor of New Orleans, Joseph Shakspeare, wrote a note to Mrs. Davis, saying: "While the entire South claims him as her own, New Orleans asks that Jefferson Davis be laid to rest within the city where he fell asleep." That note was followed by one from the president of the Metairie Cemetery Association inviting her to inter her husband at Metairie, and she accepted.

The funeral was set for December 11. Meanwhile Davis' body lay in state at City Hall (now Gallier Hall) fronting Lafayette Square. New Orleans' streets were draped in black. Hotels and boardinghouses were filled with mourners who arrived by the trainload. Newspaper estimates of the number of people passing Davis' bier ranged from 50,000 to 150,000. The funeral and procession lasted four hours. Thousands marched behind the cortege—Confederate veterans, generals and soldiers. Also, there were 30 aged veterans of the Mexican War and 15 Union soldiers then living in Louisiana.

The Episcopal bishop who conducted the service wound up by saying: "We here consign the body of Jefferson Davis, a servant of his state and country as a soldier in their armies; sometime member of Congress, Senator from Mississippi, and Secretary of War of the United States; the first and only President of the Confederate States of America; born in Kentucky on the third of June, 1808, died in Louisiana on the sixth of December, 1889, and buried here by the reverent hands of his people."

The Moriarity monument in Metairie Cemetery. Photo by A. J. Meek.

Davis' widow anguished over whether to leave his body there or move it to another state. She was persuaded finally to move it to Richmond, Virginia, capital of the Confederacy, where in May, 1893, Davis' body was reinterred in Hollywood Cemetery. The vault in Metairie which had held Davis' body was sealed forever.

Memorial art forms are at their best in Metairie. It is the final resting place for nine governors of Louisiana, seven mayors of New Orleans, three Confederate generals, four chief justices of the Louisiana Supreme Court, forty-nine kings of Carnival and countless queens (difficult to document because all of them changed names when married), and a cross section of the citizenry. General Richard ("Dick") Taylor, son of President Zachary Taylor, rests in Metairie. Taylor was one of three Confederates from civilian life who attained the rank of lieutenant general. He was a brilliant tactician. Another Confederate general buried in Metairie is John B. Hood, who commanded the Army of Tennessee for a time.

Also, Metairie contains the remains of Josie Arlington, madam of the old New Orleans red-light district, Storyville, where prostitution flourished from 1897 until 1917, when the federal government closed it during World War I. Born Mamie Deubler in Carrollton, Josie took the name of Arlington from a famous saloon, The Arlington, run by Tom Anderson, himself a legendary figure during pre-Prohibition days.

Josie was laid to rest in a handsome tomb of polished red granite. Soon, the tomb began giving off flashes of red light nightly, creating a mystery that attracted crowds. A beacon had been erected in the then existing nearby New Basin Canal, and as it swung around to warn boaters of danger it reflected on the polished granite of Josie's tomb. The mystery was short-lived because the crowds became a nuisance and the canal management had the signal light removed. Still, her tomb continued to attract an unusual number of sightseers. Her remains eventually were moved to a vault in an undisclosed location in the cemetery.

Unlike other cemeteries where burials are limited to persons of one faith or fraternal membership, Metairie is open to all. Its tombs, vaults, and graves contain the remains of Catholics, Protestants, and Jews—the rich and the powerful, and the average citizen.

Greenwood

Greenwood Cemetery, situated at Canal Boulevard, an extension of Canal Street, and City Park Avenue, is one of the larger burial sites. Founded in 1852, it became the principal burying place for New Orleans at that time, and today still records hundreds of burials each year through a system of reusing graves when bodies have disintegrated. Greenwood's plots are small; nevertheless, the cemetery has many imposing monuments. Among the more than twenty thousand burial locations, there are a number of attention-grabbing memorials.

As you enter, you see the Confederate monument bearing the likenesses in marble of Generals Robert E. Lee, Stonewall Jackson, Leonidas Polk, and Albert Sidney Johnston. The life-size statue of a volunteer fireman occupies a prominent position, as does the grassy mound tomb of the Benevolent and Protective Order of Elks, which features an elk standing alertly on top and surveying an expanse of tombs. One of the historic monuments here is erected to the memory of A. D. Crossman, mayor of New Orleans from 1846 to 1854, during which time the city experienced the severe 1853 yellow fever epidemic.

Cypress Grove

New Orleans volunteer firemen desired a special burial place to honor their dead. This led to the founding of Cypress Grove Cemeteries Nos. 1 and 2. No. 1 is located at the end of Canal Street at what once was the edge of Metairie Bayou. No. 2, near Greenwood, lasted only nine years, until the land was needed for new streets.

Cypress Grove, generally known as the Firemen's Cemetery, was founded in 1840 and is still in use. Perhaps its most interesting monument is that memorializing Irad Ferry, a businessman and fireman who lost his life January 1, 1837, in a Camp Street fire. His body was interred in Girod Cemetery, but was moved to Cypress Grove. His death is believed to have been the inspiration for the city's firefighters to establish a cemetery of their own. The Ferry monument consists of a tomb and Doric column which appears to have been broken, to symbolize a life cut short.

Cypress Grove became the main burying ground for many Protestant families when Girod Cemetery began to deteriorate. Many of the tombs match in style and architecture those of the earlier cemeteries and include some masterpieces.

Lafayette Nos. 1 and 2

Lafayette Cemetery No. 1, located in the square bounded by Washington, Prytania, Coliseum, and Sixth, was originally part of the Livaudais plantation. It was established in the early 1830s. One of the founders of the public school system, Samuel Jarvis Peters, is buried here. The cemetery contains the remains of many victims of yellow fever epidemics of the 1850s and earlier years.

The city of Lafayette was a separate municipality when the cemetery was established, and many Irish and German immigrants who lived in the area were buried here, along with a number of Civil War veterans, including Confederate General Harry T. Hays. The cast-iron gates are considered excellent examples of ironwork found in New Orleans. The city of New Orleans took over operation of Lafayette Nos. 1 and 2 in 1852, when the area was annexed to the city. Lafayette No. 2 is located on Washington Avenue between Sixth, Saratoga, and Loyola streets. It is in poor condition, time, weather, and neglect having taken a heavy toll.

St. Vincent de Paul Nos. 1, 2, and 3

St. Vincent de Paul No. 1 contains some rows of large family tombs and hundreds of small, plain tombs. The cemetery, founded in 1844, is said to have been established by a priest and at one time run by a Spanish duelist. The three cemeteries are located in the 1300 and 1400 blocks of Louisa Street.

Another St. Vincent, located at 1950 Soniat Street and operated by the Archdiocese of New Orleans, is the St. Vincent de Paul Soniat Cemetery.

St. Patrick Nos. 1, 2, and 3

Actually, this is one cemetery with three sections. Founded in 1841 by the vestry of St. Patrick's Church, they are located in the Canal Street–City Park Avenue area.

In August of 1853, during one of the catastrophic yellow fever epidemics, more than 1,100 persons were buried here. The haste necessary to arrange burial plots led to irregular development, resulting in jagged rows of graves and tombs. St. Patrick No. 2 has a number of noteworthy religious monuments. Sculptured stations of the cross stand at the entrances to these cemeteries. The St. Patrick group is managed by the Archdiocese of New Orleans. No. 3 is used principally for burial of members of religious orders.

Odd Fellows Rest

This cemetery takes its name from the Independent Order of Odd Fellows, who founded it in the Canal Street cemetery complex in 1847. It was the scene of an unusual funeral procession in 1849, when it was dedicated. A "Funeral car" bearing the remains of sixteen deceased members of the organization previously buried elsewhere was pulled by six fine horses to new gravesites.

Odd Fellows Rest contains a number of interesting memorials, but it is plagued by vandals. Its cast-iron gates represent some of the finest work to be found, but they gradually are falling victim to neglect and destruction.

St. Joseph Nos. 1 and 2

St. Joseph Nos. 1 and 2 are located in the 2200 block of Washington Avenue. No. 1 was established in 1854 to provide a place for burial of German immigrants. It was filled in less than twenty years, thus No. 2 was established, using another city square. A distinguishing feature of No. 1 is the original chapel of St. Mary Assumption Parish, one of the oldest buildings in Uptown New Orleans, dating from 1844. St. Joseph No. 2 contains a miniature Gothic chapel which once was the tomb for Redemptorist priests.

St. Roch Nos. 1, 2, and 3

St. Roch No. 1 possesses one of the most imposing entrances in the city. Built in 1874 in tribute to St. Roch, one of the Church's "Holy Helpers," the cemetery was modeled after the famous Campo Santo dei Tedeschi near St. Peter's in Rome. It contains a Gothic chapel built by a priest who vowed to construct it if members of his congregation were spared death during a yellow fever epidemic. This cemetery is a favorite shrine of the faithful today. On Good Fridays, dozens of Catholics pray at the chapel's stations of the cross. St. Roch No. 2 is an extension.

St. John

The St. John Lutheran congregation founded St. John Cemetery in 1867. It is located in the 4800 block of Canal Street and is the second Protestant cemetery to be established in New Orleans. This cemetery possesses some of the handsomest tombs to be found in the city, and in recent years its operators have established a large, modern mausoleum. Hope Mausoleum, modeled after ones on the West Coast, was built in 1931.

The cemetery and mausoleum, operated by one of the pioneer families in New Orleans cemetery management, contain the remains of some of the persons originally buried in Girod Cemetery.

Algiers Cemeteries

St. Bartholomew and St. Mary cemeteries are the most prominent in Algiers, across the river from the New Orleans business district. St. Bartholomew, located on Newton, Diana, and Nunez streets, was begun in 1849. When it became overcrowded in the early 1860s, St. Mary was built in the same area.

For many years, the pioneer Duverjé family of Algiers had its own cemetery. It occupied a city block, but fell victim to progress in the early 1900s. It was demolished, its four hundred bodies moved, and the site became a playground.

Jewish Cemeteries

The first Jewish cemetery was built in New Orleans in 1828 by Jews of German descent who had come here shortly after the Louisiana Purchase (1803). It was located in what then was the city of Lafayette, and it lasted until 1957. All remains were removed to Hebrew Rest Cemetery in Gentilly, just off Gentilly Road on Elysian Fields Avenue.

Spanish and Portuguese Jews in 1846 organized the second Jewish burial ground, in the 4900 block of Canal Street. It is the Dispersed of Judah tract.

The Jewish cemeteries contain some unusual ironwork and monuments. A hardware dealer who headed the Lighthouse for the Blind is memorialized by a miniature lighthouse in the Gates of Prayer Cemetery in the 4800 block of Canal. This burial ground was founded by a group of Polish Jews who later disbanded. Other Jewish cemeteries of note are Beth Israel, Chivra Thilim, Ahavas Sholam, Anshe Sfard, and the Jewish Burial Rites.

Chalmette National Cemetery

Part of the site of the Battle of New Orleans in Chalmette, some six miles below Canal Street, contains the U.S. National Cemetery. General Andrew Jackson and his troops defeated General Edward Pakenham and his redcoats on January 8, 1815, two weeks after the treaty ending the war had been signed in Ghent, Belgium.

The Chalmette cemetery was founded during the Civil War. Some 14,000 Union soldiers are buried here, simple white crosses marking their graves. A short distance below the cemetery is a grand avenue of oak trees, known as the Pakenham oaks, although they did not exist when the British general attacked New Orleans.

Alas, the large tombs in New Orleans' cemeteries make good hiding places for robbers. Police warn that people visiting the cemeteries should go in groups. Individuals and small parties should arrange for protection.

Graveyard Artifacts Attract Thieves

New Orleans' architecturally beautiful cemetery ornaments attracted thieves as well as tourists during the mid-1990s. When wrought-iron decorations, marble urns, and statues began disappearing from some of the historic cemeteries, police launched an investigation that resulted in rounding up a theft ring. The robbers were found to have sold their stolen items to antique dealers in New Orleans, New York, and Los Angeles. At least four men were convicted or pled guilty in criminal court and were fined or sent to prison.

W.G.C.

BIBLIOGRAPHY

Coleman, Will H. *Historical Sketchbook—Guide to New Orleans.* New York, 1884.

Gandolfo, Henri A. *Metairie Cemetery: An Historical Memoir.* New Orleans, 1981.

Huber, Leonard V. "Cities of the Dead." *New Orleanian Magazine,* October 18, 1930.

Huber, Leonard V.; Peggy McDowell; and Mary Louise Christovich. *New Orleans Architecture.* Vol. III, *The Cemeteries.* Gretna, 1974.

Strode, Hudson. *Jefferson Davis, American Patriot.* New York, 1955.

Wilson, Samuel, Jr. *A Guide to Architecture of New Orleans, 1699–1959.* New York, 1959.

Writers' Project, Works Progress Administration. *Louisiana: A Guide to the State.* American Guide Series. New York, 1941.

6.

❧ THE WEST BANK ❧

The sun does indeed rise over the west bank of the Mississippi River at New Orleans and the quaint and historic communities which line its bank. Stretched along a twenty-seven-mile strip of that bank are some 200,000 inhabitants of Algiers, Gretna, Harvey, Marrero, and Westwego. Although Algiers is the only one of these communities that is part of New Orleans—it is the city's Fifteenth Ward—the others are integral parts of the metropolitan area. The Mississippi, as with New Orleans, has been the lifeline of their commerce and the scene of many exciting events.

When New Orleans was laid out, Bienville reserved for himself a tract across the river on the West Bank. John Law's Company of the Indies established the Company Plantation, later the King's Plantation, in the same area. Algiers sprang up and developed on the Bienville and Law holdings.

After several decades of changing land ownership, Algiers came into its own in 1805 with the acquisition from Martial Le Beuf by Barthélemy Duverjé of much of the land which today makes up the Fifteenth Ward of New Orleans. Duverjé gave the West Bank area its first mansion with the construction of a plantation home in 1812. It was on Patterson Street overlooking the river where today stands the major landmark of the area—the Algiers Court House. The original Duverjé home had served as a courthouse, following Duverjé's death, but it was destroyed in the great Algiers fire of

1895. Duverjé's successful real estate ventures led to the development of many of the family-named hamlets of the Algiers–West Bank area such as Mossyville, Olivierville, Belleville, McDonoghville, Hendeeville, Leesville, Plaisanceville—in addition to Tunisburg, Cut Off, Aurora, and Stanton.

Much speculation surrounds the origin of the name Algiers. There are several legends regarding its adoption. Perhaps the most acceptable one is that suggested by William H. Seymour in *The Story of Algiers, 1718–1896*. He states that one of Alexander O'Reilly's soldiers who had participated in a campaign against Algeria gave it the name. Little credence should be given the legend linking it to Commodore Stephen Decatur's 1815 victory over the notorious Barbary pirates on the North African coast around Algiers and Tunis. Regardless of the legend surrounding its naming, the Mississippi River gives the community its character and unity, making possible its commerce, in the way of shipbuilding, ship repair, barging, warehousing, railroading, and waterborne transportation. The river figured prominently in the founding of the city, and the floods that devastated the area led to the building of the reinforced levees and inland drainage canals.

For the modern-day visitor, the Mississippi River holds many attractions. The stern-wheelers which churn up and down the river and the leisure craft that cruise the inland waterways and neighboring bayous give the visitor a closeup view of river life and important landmarks along its banks. Much can also be seen of the waterborne commerce: large oil drilling platforms being towed to exploration areas in the Gulf of Mexico and elsewhere; large grain ships carrying the Midwest's crop to all areas of the world; cruise ships; powerful tugs pushing clusters of barges, many with tons of coal destined for foreign ports.

But for all its positive attributes, the river also has wreaked havoc on the area and towns lining its banks. Major floods visited the area in 1865, 1884, 1892, 1922, and 1927, laying waste many homes, plantations, farms, and businesses. And with the floods many crevasses (levee breaks) left marks on the landscape. The

David Crockett Fire Co., No. 1, in Gretna, is the oldest volunteer fire company in the nation. Photo by A. J. Meek.

flood of May 6, 1865, according to the *Picayune* news account, devoured "a section of Algiers riverfront 300 yards long and 50 yards deep which caved in and fell with a resounding splash." The article continued: "There is sixty feet of water where there had been dry land the day before."

When Pakenham launched his major attack on Andrew Jackson's Chalmette line on January 8, 1815, his plan included an attack on the West Bank. He expected the troops assigned to this operation to capture the American position and turn its artillery on Jackson's line across the river, thus placing it under enfilading fire as well as a frontal attack. The British West Bank assault, while successful, was late getting under way, and by the time the American breastworks below Algiers were carried, Pakenham's attack had failed and the ill-starred British general was dead. General Samuel

Gibbs was mortally struck, General John Keane was severely wounded, and General John Lambert, fourth in the line of command, accepted defeat. He retired to the British position and recalled the troops on the West Bank.

Two historic Algiers figures stand out because of their contributions in education and politics. John McDonogh, who died in 1850, remains one of the city's leading philanthropists, an especial benefactor of public education. Born in Baltimore, Maryland, in 1779, he came to New Orleans in 1800 to represent a merchant from his native city. He was highly successful in his business endeavors and at one time in his career was regarded as one of Louisiana's richest men. He moved to Algiers in 1817, acquiring the beautiful plantation home Monplaisir as his residence. It was destroyed in the crevasse which inundated a large portion of Algiers Point in December of 1861. At one time he owned 610,000 acres of land and at his death had an estate valued at $2,079,926. Most of his estate was left to the cities of Baltimore and New Orleans to build public schools. Thirty-six of these in New Orleans bore his name at one time. Although McDonogh was buried in Algiers in the McDonoghville cemetery, his remains were removed in 1860 to Baltimore in conformity with his will.

The political contribution came from Martin Behrman, who served the city of New Orleans as mayor for seventeen years, the longest tenure of any mayor thus far. He served four consecutive terms from 1904 to 1920 and was elected to a fifth term in 1925, dying in office a year later. Born in New York in 1864, he was brought to New Orleans by his parents when he was seven months old. He lost his father at the age of twelve, and at the age of twenty-one he married Julia Collins. Following his marriage, he moved to Algiers, which was to become his permanent residence, and entered the mercantile business. His residence at 228 Pelican Avenue in Algiers Point where he died is still occupied today. Much has been said about his political life, but what is most remembered is his affection for the citizens he governed, which they reciprocated.

Of all the events that affected the face and fortunes of Algiers, the most devastating was the Sunday morning fire of October 20,

1895. It virtually wiped out the community. Some 250 homes were destroyed, including the old Duverjé plantation home, which was then the Algiers Court House. Amazingly, not one life was lost.

For the many who viewed the fire from the east side in the predawn hours of October 20, few could believe their eyes when dawn revealed nothing more than barren chimneys and smoldering ruins. The cause of the conflagration was never determined.

The great fire triggered an event which could have been as disastrous when several thousand spectators took to the ferry landing the following day to view the ruins. The New Orleans *Times-Democrat* of October 21 recorded the event with these headlines: "Ferry Landing Sinks" . . . "An Event That Nearly Rivaled the Big Fire" . . . "Men and Women Received Painful Injuries" . . . "Crowds Precipitated into Shallow Part of River." It happened at 6:00 P.M. when curiosity-seeking citizens, taxing the capacity of the footbridge leading from the ferry to the pontoon bridge, caused it to collapse. Men, women, and children screaming and crying in despair were thrown into the river. It was indeed a miracle that no lives were lost. The many deeds of heroism were largely responsible for the avoidance of serious tragedy.

The industrial history of Algiers and the West Bank is identified principally with railroads and shipbuilding. The Sequin shipyard was opened in 1819 by André Sequin, a native of Le Havre, France. The site was at a bend of the river opposite the French Market, at the head of the street which still bears his name. Following a very active role in the construction and repair of ships during the Civil War, the Algiers shipbuilding industry boasted a total of twenty dry docks by 1881. It was here that the tugboat *Enoch Train* was converted into the Civil War's first ironclad warship, the *Manassas*, which participated valiantly in the futile struggle with Farragut's fleet off Forts Jackson and St. Philip. Here, also, the passenger ship *Habana* was converted into the Confederate raider, the *Sumter*. Under the command of Captain Raphael Semmes, the *Sumter* recorded many daring exploits during the Civil War, including the capture of eighteen vessels and the burning of seven others.

With the rapid development of New Orleans as a major port city, Algiers became the center of much shipbuilding and ship repair work. Many of the famous stern-wheelers were launched here. It was the berthing area for the giant railcar carriers which shuttled freight and passenger cars across the Mississippi River at several points.

Of equal importance in the industrial and economic life of Algiers and the West Bank were the railroads and their repair shops. Hundreds of families derived their livelihood from railroad operations during the period from 1852 through the early 1950s. Although limited operations continue today, they do not compare to the booming operations of the Southern Pacific Railroad and its predecessor, the New Orleans, Opelousas and Great Western. The inaugural service began in 1853 with the NOO&GW seventeen-mile passenger run from Algiers westward to St. Charles Parish. Five years later this run was extended to Brashear City—now Morgan City, Louisiana—and connected with tracks through Texas leading to California. Many of the giant iron horses that traveled this route were constructed and maintained in the twenty-two-block-long Opelousas Avenue yards of the Southern Pacific.

The early success of the railroad venture was due to the interest and financial backing of Charles Morgan and the Morgan Steamship Line, which acquired the NOO&GW line in 1865 and renamed it the Morgan, Louisiana and Texas. It later became the property of the Southern Pacific, and Algiers became the eastern terminus of its Louisiana-to-California rail system, on which today travels the popular Amtrak Sunset Limited.

One cannot study and record the history of this area without giving recognition, limited as it may be, to the plantation homes that graced the mighty river's banks. All have perished due to the ravages of time, fire, and the rampaging river—save Aurora. It can be viewed from the River Road (public tours are not allowed) as one travels the right descending bank about seven miles downstream from the Canal Street ferry crossing. Notable among the extinct plantations are Leonard, Stanton, Cazelard, Point Beca, Upper Magnolia, and Fort St. Leon near English Turn, where now are sited Tulane University's Hébert Center and a U.S. Coast Guard station. Stanton was built in 1822, and Cazelard served as headquarters for American forces on the West Bank during the Battle of New Orleans.

Algiers Naval Station

One of the oldest and most prominent landmarks in the Algiers area is the naval station which bears its name. Two miles downstream from the West Bank–Canal Street ferry, the station occupies 193 acres and three-fourths of a mile of river frontage. The main entrance is located in the 2300 block of General Meyer Avenue.

The original site was acquired in 1849, but it was not until 1901 with the arrival of the navy dry dock that the station was officially designated a U.S. naval station. The following year $4 million was appropriated by Congress for new buildings and improvements. During World Wars I and II, the Algiers base became a major center for training navy personnel. In addition, it served as a base for outfitting and repairing ships.

The station is now known as Naval Support Activity–New Orleans and houses the operations of several components of the navy and marines. Those components include the Naval Reserve Professional Development Center; Naval Support Activity, New Orleans; Navy Exchange Detachment; Navy-Marine Relief Society; Naval Personnel Support Detachment; Navy Supervisor of Shipbuilding, Conversion, and Repair; Naval Legal Service, New Orleans Detachment; Naval Medical Clinic, New Orleans; Human Resource Office, New Orleans; and Headquarters 8th Marine Corps District.

These ten military units have a combined payroll of $41.3 million with a total personnel of 984 as of year end 1998.

With the opening of the new Mississippi River bridge connecting the West Bank with downtown New Orleans in 1958 and a companion span in 1989, the West Bank became an important segment of the Greater New Orleans region. Another major factor in the growth of the area is the elevated West Bank Expressway (U.S. 90 Business), stretching from the Mississippi Crescent City bridge to ground level at Westwego. Completed in 1998, this eight-mile elevated roadway represents an estimated $240 million investment.

The West Bank stretching from Algiers to Highway 90 had an estimated population of 193,394 at the end of 1998.

O.K.L.

BIBLIOGRAPHY

Dixon, Richard R. *Algiers: The Centennial Year.* New Orleans, 1970.
———. *Old Algiers.* Gretna, 1980.
Swanson, Betsy. *Historic Jefferson Parish, from Shore to Shore.* Gretna, 1975.

7.

❧ THE SUBURBS ❧

A number of communities in Jefferson Parish border New Orleans. These include Gretna, Harvey, Marrero, and Westwego on the west bank of the Mississippi River, upriver from Algiers, and Harahan, Kenner, and Metairie on the east bank. The history of the communities and the lives of their people are closely tied to New Orleans and its heritage.

Gretna

Gretna was founded in 1836 as Mechanickham, or Mechanic's Village. Land transactions date back to 1790, when the Ursuline nuns received a land grant. Nicolas Noel Destrehan subdivided the area and made provisions for a foundry, ferry, and a common, which later was named Huey P. Long Avenue. Gretna derives its name from the play *Gretna Green,* in which a non-minister performs quick marriages. A local justice of the peace was so known in 1837 when the play was put on in New Orleans. Gretna, the parish seat, was incorporated in 1913. It is a noted tourist destination. Visitors love to explore the large National Historic Register District with its unique architecture of a German settlement. Population, 17,423.

Harvey

A growing community just upriver from Gretna, Harvey was the seat of Jefferson Parish government from 1874 to 1884. The town was named for Joseph Hale Harvey, who installed a system of locks along what today is the Harvey Industrial Canal. At one time a major timber outlet, Harvey has attracted dozens of small industries along its canal. Population, 22,226.

Marrero

Named for Louis H. Marrero, one of Jefferson Parish's foremost political figures, Marrero began in the late nineteenth century as Amesville. Largely residential, the town boasts two landmarks, Madonna Manor and Hope Haven, Catholic vocational schools for young people. The institutions' buildings are known as outstanding examples of Spanish Revival Colonial architecture. Population, 36,165.

Westwego

A few surviving families of an 1893 hurricane at Chenière Caminada on the Gulf of Mexico became the early settlers of Westwego. Prior to being named Westwego, the town was known as Salaville, after Pablo Sala, who had acquired a plantation site along the Mississippi River in 1892. It was renamed by a railroad's board of directors in New York in response to the suggestion that this was the ideal spot to begin the tracks to the west. The reply, "Then *west we go* from there," gave the town its name. Westwego, which boasts it is the only town in the U.S. whose name is a complete sentence, was incorporated as a village in 1919 and as a city in 1951. Population, 11,290.

Harahan

Named for James T. Harahan, president of the Illinois Central Railroad, Harahan was incorporated in 1920. The area was the site of a demonstration farm owned by Southern University. In 1914 a group of railroad people bought the farm and cut it into residential tracts. It is primarily a bedroom community for New Orleans. Population, 9,885.

Kenner

Kenner was developed in the latter half of the nineteenth century when Belle Grove plantation was subdivided by its owner, Minor Kenner, eldest son of William Kenner, who came from Virginia to settle in the area in the late eighteenth century. He became a wealthy merchant. His sons, Minor, William Butler, Duncan Farrar, and George R., all became large landholders. Minor Kenner's plantation, divided into residential tracts, became Kennerville and then Kenner, which became a city in 1952. Population, 70,517.

Metairie

Farming along the old Metairie Ridge, built up by waters of Metairie Bayou, began about 1720 by French settlers. The bayou, no longer in existence, had for ages deposited rich soil for farming, during flooding. The early settlers rented out land to sharecroppers, and this led to the name Metairie, which in French means "small farms." Metairie today is principally a residential community with large areas of handsome homes and picturesque trees, shrubs, and flowers. Population, 146,136.

O.K.L.

Part II

The People and Their History

8.

🙢 THE PEOPLE 🙠

Long before the term *melting pot* was used to describe America and its many ethnic strains, New Orleans was the nation's first melting pot. Long before the slogan-makers labeled New Orleans the International City, New Orleans was an international city.

This became evident to Americans shortly after the Louisiana Purchase, those who flocked to the city and those who only read about it in *The Western Gazetteer or Emigrant's Directory* for the year 1817. This handbook for prospective settlers said of New Orleans: "Here in half an hour you can see, and speak to Frenchmen, Spaniards, Danes, Swedes, Germans, Englishmen, Portuguese, Hollanders, Mexicans, Kentuckians, Tennesseans, Ohioans, Pennsylvanians, New Yorkers, New Englanders and a motley group of Indians, quadroons, Africans, etc." The first people on the site of New Orleans were the Choctaw Indians, about whom a French missionary said: "Before we can make Christians of these savages, we must first make them human beings."

There is no evidence that Cabeza de Vaca and the remnants of the Pánfilo de Narváez expedition passed in the immediate vicinity of the future New Orleans in their long trek through the wilderness to Mexico in 1536. But Luis de Moscoso floated past the site in 1543 with survivors of Hernando de Soto's expedition, after the leader died near present-day Memphis. Accordingly, the first Europeans, the Spanish, on Louisiana soil had nothing to do with New

Orleans, which was then almost two centuries away from its establishment. And the day of Spanish rule in New Orleans was yet another half century further away.

It remained for the French to claim and settle Louisiana and establish New Orleans, but all this didn't even begin to take place until almost a century and a half after Moscoso's improvised boats floated past the great crescent in the river where New Orleans would ultimately be founded. René Robert Cavelier, Sieur de La Salle, descended the Mississippi to its mouth in 1682 and on April 9 claimed all the land drained by the great river and its tributaries for Louis XIV, naming it Louisiane, meaning the realm, the domain of Louis. The "committee" that heard La Salle make his formal proclamation—the band with which he had descended the river—had an international flavor: twenty-one Frenchmen, the Italian Henri de Tonty, eighteen Mohegan and Abnaki Indians, ten of whom brought their families, along with three children.

France did nothing to implement La Salle's claim for a dozen years after his murder in 1687 during his abortive second expedition to establish a French settlement in Louisiana. It was not until the fall of 1698 that Pierre Le Moyne, Sieur d'Iberville, sailed from Brest with four vessels for Louisiana. Twenty years later Iberville's younger brother, Jean-Baptiste Le Moyne, Sieur de Bienville, established New Orleans.

The quality of most of the French colonists in the early years of Louisiana was not very high. One French official described them as "shiftless . . . libertines who care only to run the woods." Of the turbulent Canadian *coureurs de bois*, a missionary declared: "Without faith or law, drunkards and blasphemers, these young fugitives from Canada for crimes or debts lead a libertine life with the young savage girls; it is necessary to let them marry them to restrain them."

The situation didn't improve after Bienville established New Orleans in 1718, for France continued to send out criminals and other undesirables to populate the new city. As more and more unworthy colonists reached New Orleans, Bienville's impatience and irritation grew. In October, 1719, he complained bitterly: "It is very disagreeable for an officer charged with the defense of a colony to have . . . only a band of deserters, smugglers and scoundrels, who are all ready not only to abandon you but also to turn against you."

Bienville's complaint brought results. Within six months the deportation of criminals and disreputable persons to New Orleans ceased. France now looked elsewhere for colonists, and that is how stolid, hard-working German peasants were recruited for Louisiana. It is an interesting fact that the first real stability in French Louisiana was due to the arrival of German immigrants in the early 1720s. About ten thousand Germans were recruited, according to one authority, but only six thousand actually sailed for New Orleans. Disease and hardships of the long journey took a frightful toll and only about two thousand Germans actually reached Louisiana.

The inability of French officials to cope with German names resulted in the gallicizing of these names—Himmel became Hymel, Kleinpeter became Clampetre, Katzenberger became Casbergue, Edelmaier became Delmaire. The most startling transformation was that of Johann Zweig, who, when the French notary got through with him, became Jean La Branche.

Just about the time the Germans began to arrive at New Orleans, the first large shipment of Negro slaves reached the colony, when on July 7, 1720, 147 slaves disembarked. In 1721 a census was taken in New Orleans and its vicinity. Of a total of 470 men, women, and children in the city, 172 were Negroes. In the environs, there were 533 slaves among the 1,269 men, women, and children.

After the coming of the Germans and the Negroes, there were few representatives of other nationalities in New Orleans until the Spanish regime. This lasted for thirty-seven years, from March 5, 1766, when the first Spanish governor, Don Antonio de Ulloa, arrived with three civil officials and ninety soldiers, until the transfer of Louisiana back to France on November 30, 1803.

It was during the Spanish regime that the Acadians settled in Louisiana in large numbers. The French-speaking Acadians, familiarly known as Cajuns—this is a corruption of 'Cadien, itself a corruption of Acadien—began drifting into Louisiana in the closing years of the French regime. The Acadians had been expelled by the British from Nova Scotia in 1755. About fifteen hundred of them subsequently came to Louisiana and settled on the Mississippi above New Orleans and along Bayous Teche, Lafourche, and Vermilion.

In 1785 the Spanish Crown performed the greatest transatlantic movement of colonists in American colonial history. About sixteen hundred Acadians, who were among an enclave of more than three thousand who settled in France, were brought in seven ships to New Orleans. That they instilled new life in the colony is borne out by the comment of Governor Esteban Miró: "The enthusiasm, industry and loyalty of these new colonists will boost the prosperity of our province."

Upriver Americans began, in the late 1780s, floating their surplus products down the Mississippi to Spanish New Orleans for transshipment to the ports of the eastern seaboard of the United States. These Kentucky and Ohio Valley people were the first Americans to visit New Orleans in any number. But after the Louisiana Purchase, eager fortune-seekers from the East swarmed into New Orleans—brokers, merchants, traders, lawyers, doctors, frontiersmen, adventurers.

There was no ready rapport between the Americans and the native Creoles, largely of French origin, but some of Spanish. The Creoles didn't understand the Americans and the Americans didn't understand them. Virginia-born William C. C. Claiborne, appointed governor of Louisiana by President Thomas Jefferson, was himself caught up in the mutual lack of understanding. This is reflected in a letter to Jefferson:

> I believe the citizens of Louisiana are, generally speaking, honest, and that a decided majority of them are attached to the American Government. But they are uninformed, indolent, luxurious—in a word, illy fitted to be useful citizens of a Republic. Under the Spanish Government education was discouraged, and little respectability attached to science. Wealth alone gave respect and influ-

ence, and hence it has happened that ignorance and wealth so generally pervade this part of Louisiana. I have seen, sir, in this city, many youths to whom nature has been apparently liberal, but from the injustice and inattention of their parents, have no other accomplishment to recommend them but dancing with elegance and ease. The same observation will apply to the young females, with this additional remark, that they are the most handsome women in America.

A second wave of Germans reached New Orleans in the first two decades of the nineteenth century. These were called Redemptioners, because they became indentured servants for a designated period until they "redeemed" their debt to the person who had paid their passage from Germany to New Orleans. Unlike the first Germans to reach Louisiana, their names were not gallicized, and for many years they sustained their German language and customs. A third wave of Germans arrived after the 1848 disturbances in Europe and this group included intellectuals and professional men.

The potato famine in Ireland was the catalyst that sent thousands upon thousands of Irishmen to America from the 1830s on, and New Orleans received many of these indigent immigrants. However, Irishmen already were established in the city during the Spanish regime. Charles McCarthy, who came to New Orleans in 1731, remained and he became Macarty to the Creoles. In 1768, Oliver Pollock was already established in business in New Orleans, and during the American Revolution he obtained Spanish help in supplying the Continental army with powder, shot, and other matériel. Daniel Clark became a prosperous merchant and landowner, and his nephew of the same name surpassed him in wealth and influence in the last decade of Spanish rule.

An English traveler, Thomas Ashe, who visited New Orleans in 1808, noted that in trade in New Orleans, the Irish played a prominent part: "Virginians and Kentuckians reign over the brokerage and commission business; the Scotch and Irish absorb all the respectable commerce on exportation and importation; the French keep magazines [warehouses] and stores; and the Spaniards do all the small retail trade." There were enough influential Irishmen in

New Orleans—a contemporary newspaper referred to "a respectable party of Irishmen in this city"—to celebrate St. Patrick's Day for the first time in 1809. It must have been a convivial affair, for seventeen toasts were proposed and drunk.

As the American Civil War neared, New Orleans took on the aspect of an international city in a way probably unmatched in any other city, New York, perhaps, excepted. The census of 1860 revealed that more than thirty-two nations were represented among 155,000 nonblacks and that 41 percent of the people were foreign-born. The 23,000 Irish and 19,000 Germans headed the list.

In the closing years of the nineteenth century, Italian immigrants began to arrive in New Orleans in great numbers. By the 1980s, a large segment of New Orleans' population was of Italian origin There is also a sizable number of Yugoslavs. Since World War II and, more specifically, since Fidel Castro's rise in Cuba, the Latin American population of New Orleans has skyrocketed. There are perhaps eighty thousand Latin Americans living in the city.

In the latter part of the twentieth century there was an influx of Asians, especially from Vietnam following the conflict in which the U.S. was engaged. The Vietnamese spread across the city, but especially gathered in the eastern section, claiming at first mostly low-paying jobs but later expanding their skills to open restaurants and a number of other kinds of businesses.

This survey of the multiplicity of peoples who have contributed to the traditions of New Orleans would not be complete without an explanation of the term *Creole*. The Spanish, in the early days of the sixteenth century, used the word *criollo* to designate a pure-blooded Spanish child born in the New World, distinct from mestizo, the offspring of a Spanish father and an Indian mother, and from mulatto, the child of a Spanish father and a Negro mother.

The term *criollo* was borrowed by the French in the West Indies and changed to Créole, to designate a child born to French parents—indeed to European parents—in the French islands and

Louisiana. In its early years, New Orleans had Créoles of French, Spanish, and German origin. A century later, Governor Henry Johnson, born of English parents in Louisiana, claimed that he was a Créole, and nobody challenged him. Technically, the term *Créole* was applicable only to the first generation, but it became loosely used to describe descendants of Créoles as well. Thus, it is customary for one whose family descended from a first-generation Créole, perhaps as far back as two hundred years, to consider himself a Créole.

Louisianians came in time not only to use Créole as a noun, but to employ the word, with a small *c,* as an adjective to describe anything indigenous—hence créole tomatoes, cabbage, peppers, eggs; also a créole mule or a créole Negro. An auctioneer's description of a slave as a créole Negro indicated to potential buyers that the slave spoke French, whereas an American Negro spoke English and an African Negro spoke neither. It is not difficult to appreciate how confusion arose outside of Louisiana, with many believing that a Créole had mixed blood. Further complications crept into this concept when French-speaking *gens de couleur libres,* free people of color, were considered Créoles. Today, some of their descendants still identify themselves as Créoles.

C.L.D.

BIBLIOGRAPHY

Carter, Clarence E., ed. *Territorial Papers of the United States,* IX. Washington, D.C., 1940.

Dufour, Charles L. *New Orleans: The Crescent City.* New York, 1967.

———. *Ten Flags in the Wind.* New York, 1967.

Huber, Leonard V. *New Orleans: A Pictorial History.* New York, 1971.

King, Grace. *New Orleans: The Place and the People.* New York, 1895.

9.

 EIGHTEENTH CENTURY

The first revolt of an American colony against a European country occurred in New Orleans in 1768, seven years before the shot heard 'round the world was fired at Lexington to open the Revolution. New Orleans' rebels ended up before a firing squad or in prison, and Louisiana remained a colony long after English America was free. Yet the conspirators were hailed as martyrs, and their executioner damned with the epithet "Bloody." The uprising was a climactic event in the years between the establishment of a French settlement at New Orleans in 1718 and the acquisition of the Louisiana Territory by the United States in 1803.

By a secret treaty signed at Fontainebleau on November 3, 1762, Louis XV of France ceded Louisiana to his Bourbon cousin, Charles III of Spain. The pact was not publicized in Paris until April 21, 1764, and Louisianians did not learn of their new masters until October of that year, when Jean-Jacques Blaise d'Abbadie, director and commandant of the colony, made the announcement. The stunned French settlers sent the wealthy Jean Milhet to Paris to try to persuade Louis XV to change his mind. The emissary did not even get to see the king.

Charles III was in no hurry to claim his gift, and the colonists had begun to hope that perhaps Louisiana would remain French, but on July 10, 1765, Don Antonio de Ulloa sent word from Havana that he had been named governor and would be coming to take over. He did not reach New Orleans until March 5, 1766, and when he disembarked he had only three civil officials and ninety Spanish soldiers with him. Ulloa did little to win the hearts of the hostile New Orleanians. He spent one eight-month period at the Balize, at the mouth of the Mississippi, awaiting the arrival of his Peruvian bride-to-be, and then was married in a private ceremony there rather than in a public wedding in New Orleans at which the populace could make merry. An economic crisis resulted in devalued French currency, and Ulloa was short of official funds. Under the circumstances, Ulloa elected to delay asserting Spanish authority until he had reinforcements for his troops. Meanwhile, the colony was governed by Charles Philippe Aubry, d'Abbadie's successor, who carried out instructions given to him by Ulloa in accordance with his orders from Paris to cooperate with the new regime.

Insurrection was brewing, and a cabal of prominent colonists made plans to drive Ulloa away. One of the conspirators was Nicolas Denis Foucault, the French commissary. Foucault was having an affair with Marie Louise de Pradel, widow of Chevalier Jean Pradel, and the group met at her home. Others in the plot included Nicolas Chauvin de Lafrenière, attorney general; Jean and Joseph Milhet; Pierre Caresse; Joseph Petit; Pierre Poupet; Balthasar Mazan; Pierre Marquis; Jean-Baptiste Noyan and his brother, Noyan-Bienville, grandnephews of Bienville; Joseph Roy Villeré; Julien Jérôme Doucet; and Pierre Hardy de Boisblanc.

By mid-October the group learned that the Spanish were assembling troops in Havana to send to Ulloa. The time had come to act. A memorial asking Ulloa's expulsion was circulated in the colony. The ringleader, Lafrenière, and the others managed to stir up the German planters who had settled on the German Coast, on the river above New Orleans, and the Acadians along the bayous to the west. The Germans were told that Ulloa would not pay them for grain purchased by the Spanish, and the Acadians were made to believe that Ulloa planned to sell them for slaves.

The first open act of rebellion occurred on October 25. Ulloa had learned that the Germans were being incited, and sent Gilbert St.

Maxent to them with funds to pay the debt. The conspirators intercepted and held St. Maxent. Ulloa ordered Spanish military personnel aboard the Spanish frigate *Volante*, which was anchored in the river, and gave instructions for the destruction of official papers.

Aubry confronted Lafrenière and Foucault in a vain effort to persuade them to call off the plot. He warned of the consequences. On October 28, contingents totaling about five hundred Germans and Acadians marched into the city to join the rebels. A thousand armed men roamed the streets. At Aubry's urging, Ulloa took refuge aboard the *Volante*. Over Aubry's protest, the Superior Council adopted a resolution citing grievances and calling for Ulloa's expulsion. On November 1, Ulloa sailed for Havana aboard the French frigate *César*, the *Volante* not being seaworthy.

The day of reckoning was coming for the conspirators, alternately described as French patriots who would risk death rather than live under another flag and as adventurers who were driven to revolt because they were hurt financially by a Spanish ban on trade with French Caribbean islands. Charles III appointed Alexander O'Reilly, an Irishman who had risen to general in the Spanish army, as governor of Louisiana and ordered him to New Orleans to establish the Crown's rule and to punish the insurrectionists. On July 24, 1769, word reached New Orleans that a Spanish fleet was entering the river. Two of the conspirators, Marquis and Petit, tried to persuade the colonists to resist the landing. Petit, holding pistols, threatened to shoot anybody who would not join him. When only a few score responded, Marquis and Petit realized their cause was hopeless.

Aubry held a public meeting in the Place d'Armes (now Jackson Square) and warned that only prompt submission could ward off "the misfortunes with which you are now threatened." Lafrenière, Marquis, and Joseph Milhet hurried to the Balize for a meeting with O'Reilly on the new governor's vessel. Lafrenière blamed the uprising on Ulloa's harshness.

The Spanish governor Francisco Luis Hector, Baron de Carondelet, under whose governorship Louisiana received its first theater, its first newspaper, and who dug the canal that bore his name, connecting New Orleans with Lake Pontchartrain by way of Bayou St. John. The Historic New Orleans Collection.

Twenty-six hundred Spanish troops marched off twenty-four vessels when O'Reilly reached New Orleans on August 18. The French flag was lowered and the Spanish flag raised in the square. Three days later O'Reilly ordered twelve conspirators arrested. One, Joseph Villeré, was taken into custody at the city gates and on the same day, aboard a Spanish frigate, either was stabbed to death or died of a seizure. Meanwhile, notices displayed at street corners carried O'Reilly's statement that the king was convinced that inhabitants had been seduced by the intrigues of "ambitious, fanatic and evil-minded men" who alone would answer for the rebellion. After a trial in which the conspirators unwittingly gave self-incriminating evidence, O'Reilly on October 24 ordered the hanging of Lafrenière, Noyan, Caresse, Marquis, and Joseph Milhet. The others received prison sentences, which soon were commuted. Since there was no hangman in New Orleans, the five condemned Frenchmen were shot by a firing squad on October 25.

Unsympathetic early historians bestowed the name "Bloody" on O'Reilly, and so he has been called ever since. In fact, he was an excellent administrator and the first of a series of Spanish governors under whom the colony prospered as it never did during the years of French rule.

In 1721, New Orleans was a collection of about one hundred wooden huts in the canebrakes beside the mighty and capricious river. The population of the town was 470, while the suburbs had 1,269, both figures including slaves. Father Pierre F. X. Charlevoix, a missionary, could only have been regarded as a visionary when he wrote that "this savage and deserted place . . . will one day, and perhaps that day will not be distant, be a wealthy city and the metropolis of a great and rich colony." In August of 1723, Bienville officially made the town the capital of Louisiana, the colony that he ruled as commandant general for John Law's Mississippi Company.

The era in which Louisiana was a French colony would have been even bleaker had it not been for the fortuitous advent of the Germans who settled upriver and the refugee Acadians whose industry and thrift began to transform the area to the west. They provided

DON ALEXANDRE Ô REILLY,

Commandeur de Benfayan dans l'Ordre de Alcantara, Lieutenant-Général & Infpecteur-Général des Armées de Sa Majefté Catholique, Capitaine-Général & Gouverneur de la Province de la Louifianne.

POUR remedier aux grands inconveniens qui réfultent tous les jours de la facilité avec laquelle s'introduifent les Etrangers, tant dans cette Ville que dans les Habitations de la Campagne, fans en avoir obtenu la permiffion du Gouvernement.

Nous Défendons à tous les Habitans établis fur les Rives du Fleuve Milliffipy & à ceux qui habitent au Bayoa, Gentilly, Opeloußas, Atakapas, Natchitoches, & autres endroits de cette Province, de recevoir ni loger chez eux aucun Etranger fans qu'il foit porteur d'un Paffeport ou Permiffion fignée de Notre Main : Défendons auffi à tous lefdits Habitans de leur vendre, loüer ni prêter aucune Voiture, Chevaux, Chariots ni Guides, fous tel pretexte que ce foit quand même ils fe diroient ou feroient porteurs de Paquets pour Nous.

Nous permettons néanmoins aux Habitans établis fur les Rives du Fleuve de vendre leurs Légumes, Volailles, & Rafraichiffements au paffage des Batimens, pourvu qu'ils s'en faffent payer en Argent & non en Effets & qu'ils les livreront au bord de l'Eau.

Nous Défendons expreffement à qui que ce foit, de la Ville ou de la Campagne d'achetter ni traitter aucunes Marchandifes des Etrangers qui Naviguent dans le Fleuve ou dans les Lacs fans Notre Permiffion expreffe, fous peine de confifcation de tout ce qu'ils auront achetté & d'une Amende de 500. livres dont le tiers du tout fera donné au Délateur.

Donné en Notre Hôtel à la Nouvelle Orléans, le 11 Septembre 1769.

Ô Reilly

O'Reilly's proclamation, September, 1769, was one of several issued by the governor who crushed the Creole revolt against Spanish rule. The Historic New Orleans Collection.

not only agricultural products, which could be traded, but also stability that was lacking in the early settlers. Fortunately, by now the regent of France had forbidden the banishment to Louisiana of criminals and misfits who were a large proportion of the early population.

In 1724, Bienville promulgated the Code Noir (Black Code), which had been drawn up by Louis XIV's government. While designed primarily for the control of slaves in the colony, it contained provisions for the protection of the slaves from cruelty and inhuman treatment by owners. The first articles of the Code Noir decreed the expulsion of Jews from Louisiana, and the third article made Roman Catholicism the official religion, precluding all other modes of worship. A pioneering bill of rights is embodied in the fifty-fourth (last) article of the Code Noir, wherein the king granted to all freed slaves "the same rights, privileges and immunities" to which they would have been entitled had they been born free.

Slaves were an essential factor in the economic life of Louisiana throughout the French and Spanish regimes. In 1803, when Louisiana became American, the area constituting the present state of Louisiana had a population of 42,000, of which approximately half were slaves or free people of color.

Relations with the Indians were a constant problem for Bienville and his successor, Etienne de Périer. The Indians knew the only military force in the colony was small. Bienville depended upon diplomacy and guile, maneuvering one tribe against another. Agents from the English colonies on the Atlantic Coast did what they could to stir up trouble for the French.

On December 2, 1729, a few survivors reached New Orleans with the news of the massacre of about 250 French colonists at Fort Rosalie (at the site of present-day Natchez) by the Natchez tribe. Frantic residents went to work digging a moat and constructing a rampart for the defense of New Orleans. No braves came on the scene, and on January 27, 1730, Périer turned to the offensive. He sent Jean Paul Le Sueur and 500 Choctaw Indians against the Natchez. They killed 80 and put the rest to flight, rescuing 51 of the French women and children who had been captured at Fort Rosalie. In February a siege of two forts in which the Natchez holed up resulted in the release of the rest of the hostages.

The Mississippi Company surrendered its interest in the colony and on July 1, 1731, Louisiana became a crown colony. Bienville returned as governor in 1733 and resumed his efforts to settle the Indian problem. In 1736 he led an assault on three villages of the Chickasaw tribe, implacable enemies of the French. With the help of English officers and 200 English soldiers, the Indians repulsed him. In 1740 he was more successful. An attack resulted in the deaths of 36 braves and the capture of many others, and the Chickasaws agreed to make peace.

Bienville's successor, Marquis Pierre de Rigaud de Vaudreuil de Cavagnial, held power during a peaceful decade, the period from 1743 to 1753, by far the best years of the French regime. He earned his designation as Le Grand Marquis, for he captivated the colony with his elegance and busy social life. High society in New Orleans had its genesis in Vaudreuil's time, a period of relative tranquility bequeathed by the hard-working Bienville. In 1753 the marquis welcomed his successor, Louis Billouart, Chevalier de Kerlérec, with a feast to which four hundred of the elite were invited. For the soldiers and all the rest of New Orleans, two fountains of wine flowed in the Place d'Armes.

Kerlérec had to deal with new outbreaks of trouble with the Indians and a resumption of a long-standing feud between the Jesuits and the Capuchins, each of which aspired to authority in the religious life of the colony. During the Seven Years' War, New Orleans was cut off from France by English mastery of the sea. Fearful of an attack on the colony, Kerlérec once turned to the Spanish at Vera Cruz, Mexico, for ammunition. In the treaty that ended the war France lost to England Canada, all of Louisiana east of the Mississippi River except New Orleans and its immediate area, and Florida. Thus it was a Louisiana much reduced in size that Louis XV gave to Spain in the Treaty of Fontainebleau. There had been, however, far-reaching economic events during the French occupation: the introduction of cotton-growing on Louisiana plantations in 1741 and the first planting of sugarcane by the Jesuits in 1751. The New Orleans that Spain acquired was a busy port because of trade with the West Indies and the mother countries in Europe, but its true importance in the political and commercial worlds was to come later when Americans pushed westward into

Ohio, Tennessee, Kentucky, and other areas and the Mississippi River became the artery through which their economic life-blood flowed.

The Frenchmen who lived under the Spanish flag had no hesitancy in lending their efforts against the British in the American Revolution. By now the governor was a brilliant young soldier, Bernardo de Galvez, who seized Baton Rouge and Natchez from English garrisons in 1779, Mobile in 1780, and Pensacola in 1781. Galvez also supplied arms and matériel to Oliver Pollock, the American agent in New Orleans, as is related in Chapter 10.

Galvez's successor, Esteban Miró, was the go-between in strange dealings between the Spanish government and James Wilkinson, a general in the Continental army who came to New Orleans in 1787. Wilkinson plotted the separation of Kentucky from the United States and sought to promote trade between Kentucky and New Orleans. As "No. 13," the signature he used in correspondence with Miró, Wilkinson declared his intent to transfer his allegiance from the United States to Spain. He was paid two thousand pesos a year by the Spanish, and the arrangement continued even after he became commander-in-chief of the American army. It was not the last time that New Orleans was a scene of intrigue against the new American Republic. After the Louisiana Purchase the former vice-president Aaron Burr visited the city and sought confederates for his schemes. One plan that he discussed was for Louisiana to join Kentucky and other western states after they had seceded from the Union to set up a country independent of the United States. He also talked of an invasion of Spanish Mexico.

During Miró's governorship, an attempt was made to establish the Spanish Inquisition in New Orleans. Padre Antonio de Sedella arrived in 1788 after his appointment as commissary of the Inquisition. He was sent away by Miró, who did not want religious strife to shatter the amity of his administration. One of the heartwarming developments in the history of New Orleans was the return of the priest, then using the French name Père Antoine. His good works made him the best-loved cleric ever to serve in the city, and a passageway alongside St. Louis Cathedral is named Père Antoine Alley, in his honor.

The most far-reaching achievement of the Spanish during Miró's term was the importation at the expense of the government in Madrid of more than sixteen hundred Acadians who, after their expulsion from Nova Scotia and a stay in England, had languished in France. They came in 1785 in seven groups and were given land, seeds, tools, and livestock in the bayou country where other Acadian refugees had settled some twenty years earlier. The Cajuns, many of whom continue to speak French in the late twentieth century, have exerted a progressive and steadying influence on Louisiana life.

The French Revolution divided New Orleans into three camps in 1793. There were the Spanish loyalists, the adherents of the deposed Bourbons, and the sympathizers with the Republicans. Reported Governor François Louis Hector, Baron de Carondelet: "By the exertion of the utmost vigilance, and at the cost of sleepless nights, by frightening some, by punishing others, by driving several out of the colony, and particularly those Frenchmen who had latterly come among us, and who had already contaminated the greater part of the province with their notions and maxims of equality, by intercepting the letters and papers of a suspicious character, and by dissembling with all, I have obtained more than I hoped, considering the whole colony is now in a state of internal tranquility." Those driven out were six Jacobins, who were sent to prison in Havana. Revolutionary songs were sung in theaters and taverns and on the streets.

In 1794 and 1795, Etienne Boré perfected a method of granulation that revived the production of sugarcane. He made a $5,000 profit from his 1796 crop, and plantation owners who had grown indigo now produced cane instead.

In 1798 the city had its first visit from a future king. The Duc d'Orléans, who would become King Louis Philippe in 1830, arrived for a stay, accompanied by his brothers, the Duc de Montpensier and the Duc de Beaujolais. They were the great-grandsons of Philippe d'Orléans, the regent of France for whom New Orleans was named.

The Spanish were more adept administrators than the French, and a succession of qualified governors made the Spanish years productive in the colony. But events far from Louisiana shores were building up to a climax that would make New Orleans an American city.

In midland America the defeat of the English was followed by rapid development of the virgin territory. The settlers were producing vast stores of goods that would find an eager market in the Atlantic states, but the Allegheny Mountains formed a barrier. It would be much easier to send the produce down the Mississippi to New Orleans, where it could be reloaded and taken by ship to eastern ports. For a period Spain enforced an embargo, although smugglers were active. The pressures were building from frontiersmen who were ready to start shooting if necessary in order to have access to the Gulf of Mexico port. Finally, on October 27, 1795, Pinckney's Treaty between Spain and the United States established commercial relations, granted Americans free navigation of the Mississippi and the right to deposit goods in New Orleans without payment of duty. When Spain cancelled the right of deposit in 1802, President Thomas Jefferson's determination to try to acquire New Orleans led to the Louisiana Purchase.

Meanwhile, Napoleon Bonaparte, First Consul of France, had forced Spain to return Louisiana. Spain was in a poor position to resist Bonaparte's pressure. The deal was sealed by the secret Treaty of San Ildefonso on October 1, 1800.

J.W.

BIBLIOGRAPHY

Dufour, Charles L. *Ten Flags in the Wind*. New York, 1967.

10.

✤ OLIVER POLLOCK ✤

In 1972, I first learned of this forgotten founding father from an article about him in the *New Orleans Magazine*. It told how James Alton James had discovered Pollock in doing research for a book on that hero of the Ohio River valley, General George Rogers Clark. James turned up a letter from the general himself, stating he could not have waged his 1777 victorious campaign had it not been for the financial support of "Mr. Pollock of New Orleans." Clark's band of two hundred men captured settlements in Illinois and Indiana, as well as Colonel Hamilton, the British commander in the area. James, so impressed with Pollock's years-long Revolutionary War exploits, wrote a book about him, *Oliver Pollock: The Life and Times of an Unknown Patriot*. James, thus, had acquired his knowledge of Pollock by accident, and so has the writer of this chapter. I have been a Pollock fan ever since.

The conquest of the Northwest by Clark, and holding it for the duration, cannot be underestimated. It was the only American campaign west of the Alleghenies and the $91,000 Pollock paid to finance it was worth every cent. Because of it, at the peace treaty following the war, the United States claimed its western boundary extended beyond the Alleghenies to the Mississippi, and included lands north of the Ohio River.

In the accompanying illustration I have labeled this territory "Pollock Purchase," with the implication that without it there

This forgotten patriot, Oliver Pollock, provided funds for George Rogers Clark's campaign to the west, which, after the Revolution, resulted in the United States' extending its boundaries and set the stage for the Louisiana Purchase. Illustration by John C. Chase.

could never have been a Louisiana Purchase twenty years after the treaty that ended the American Revolution. Imagine Napoleon selling Louisiana to the United States, if English territory separated the two. That clearly was unthinkable. After reading James's book and everything else I could find, I became convinced Pollock was certainly the right man in the right place, and at the right time, to do America a lot of good. And he did. It is puzzling how such a man could ever become unknown and forgotten.

But he was unknown to the Cabildo in 1972, when Dr. Joseph P. Colvin's letter arrived from Memphis. Speaking for his wife, the only known descendant of Pollock, Dr. Colvin was writing to inquire if the Cabildo museum would like to have two rare mementoes of her great-great-great-great-grandfather. After all, New Orleans was where he made his great contributions to American history, Colvin added. When the Cabildo curator indicated indifference to such a donation the Colvins withdrew their offer.

I learned about this in the summer of 1975, when—in prepara-tion for the Bicentennial of the American Revolution—I had just agreed to do a Pollock cover story for the *Times-Picayune*'s Sunday Dixie magazine. I lost no time getting in touch with Dr. Colvin, who proved to be a gold mine of information on his distinguished in-law. In his years-long research, he had even spoken with Mrs. Colvin's grandfather, who, as a boy, remembered the Oliver Pol-lock portrait at his home in Bayou Sara, which the Yankee gunboat *Essex* later destroyed, along with the entire town of Bayou Sara near St. Francisville. It is from his description, as related to Colvin, that Pollock's likeness shown here was re-created.

This right man in the right place arrived in New Orleans in 1767 at age thirty-one. Five years earlier he had first set foot in the New World at Philadelphia, as did so many penniless immigrants from northern Ireland at this time. But unlike most of his country-men, who moved west into western Pennsylvania and the Ohio River valley to become America's frontiersmen, Pollock almost immediately went back to sea as a world trader. He appears to have been a well-educated young man, and not without experience as a salesman. At sea he taught himself Spanish, the better to trade in the West Indies, where he lost no time selling himself as a salesman to the leading mercantile company in Havana. Also, Pollock was a gregarious young man. He liked people, and usually the right people. Soon he was on intimate terms with the head of the Jesuit Society in Cuba, Father Thomas Murphy, as well as with General Alexander O'Reilly, who commanded the Spanish troops there. As a salesman, he was setting records, and he and Margaret O'Brien were seriously talking about marriage. Surely the future for Pollock in Havana appeared bright.

Instead, in 1767 he resigned his lucrative position, kissed Mar-garet good-bye, and, with the best wishes for Father Murphy and General O'Reilly, left the solidly built, civilized community of Havana for a wilderness settlement called New Orleans. The French and Indian War had just ended. As the winner, England was in possession of all continental North America east of the

Mississippi, and by secret treaty France had ceded that river's west bank to Spain—and had persuaded England that New Orleans was on the west bank.

Pollock had heard the talk. A thousand miles up that river from New Orleans was the world's greatest trading bonanza called the American Bottom. There trade was possible with the Indians to the west and north, and with the Ohio River settlers to the east. Even then the Mississippi River valley was being called a treasure-house, and Pollock considered it held a brighter future for him than Havana did.

But, in 1767, there was nothing about New Orleans to foretell its future as the only seaport for this golden valley. Instead, it was a bleak little community of seven hundred buildings on thirty-three squares, with vegetable gardens above, below, and behind the town. On its riverfront, a levee two feet high protected the town from flooding, backed up by twenty-four cannons aiming to protect the unattractive community from only God knew what else. The populace, less than three thousand souls, was grumbling about the impending Spanish takeover of the French colony, and there was talk of a revolt to stop it.

Pollock was too busy organizing his business to pay much attention to politics. There was need to get his boats readied with supplies and crews for next spring's departure of the usual fleet of some twenty boats for the American Bottom. For security from Indians, river pirates, and rival English trading boats, the Spanish boats traveled together for the four-month wilderness journey.

Pollock was away on a buying trip in Baltimore when the Creole revolt broke. He arrived back in New Orleans to find that his friend General O'Reilly had arrived with 2,600 troops and ended the revolt, but with so many more mouths to feed, a famine threatened. Whereupon, Pollock made available to his friend the whole shipload of flour he had just brought from Baltimore, for whatever O'Reilly wanted to pay. In appreciation for this, O'Reilly conferred upon Pollock the privilege of trading in Spanish Louisiana without payment of any taxes or fees.

That did it. Outstripping all competition, in seven years Oliver

Pollock was a merchant prince, with sufficient funds to become the fourth-largest financial contributor to the American Revolution, which had just commenced. Only the financial backing of the kingdoms of France and Spain and the Dutch bankers exceeded an estimated $300,000 Pollock made available to the American cause.

It is impossible to reckon the value of such an amount in 1776. As president, Washington did not sign the bill for a U.S. Mint until 1792. But the Spanish peso, which is the model for the U.S. dollar, was also called "dollar" in Pollock's time. A symbol for the Spanish peso, the first dollar sign—an *s* written over a *p*—has been proven by Dr. Florian Cajori to have first appeared in a letter written by Pollock to George Rogers Clark on September 12,

Oliver Pollock was the first to use the dollar sign (an *s* written over a *p*) in his letter to George Rogers Clark, September 12, 1778. Padre Cirillo, the first Spanish rector of St. Louis Church, carved this memento for Pollock; it can be seen in the Ursulines' museum on State Street. Illustration by John C. Chase.

1778. The almost immediate popularity of the dollar sign in colonial New Orleans is reflected in the picture here of the Spanish Capuchin Padre Cirillo de Barcelona, a friend of Pollock's and the first Spanish rector of St. Louis Church. He is shown with one of the two rare mementoes of Pollock rejected by the Cabildo in 1972 and accepted by the museum of the Ursuline Convent, 2635 State Street, when Mrs. Colvin donated them on August 27, 1975. Carved by Padre Cirillo for Pollock in 1779, the memento can be seen in the Ursuline museum on State Street. The other Cirillo carving is a cross.

So, it appears America's first dollar-a-year man quite by accident "invented" the dollar sign ($). It is further evident, too, that Pollock's was the first great American success story, even before there was a United States of America. Pollock's papers reveal he was personally acquainted with Washington, Franklin, Jefferson (whom he greatly resembled), Patrick Henry, and Robert Morris. This unknown founding father was certainly *very* well known to his well-known colleagues. How he escaped mention in the history books is puzzling.

Neither was he unknown to the Spaniards of his time. Spain joined the Americans in the war against England because Pollock, through Governor Bernardo de Galvez, convinced Spain it was to her best interests, and it was. In 1779 he joined Galvez's 1,424-man march on English Baton Rouge, as his aide. After its capture, he single-handedly got British-held Natchez to surrender. He simply wrote his friends there, recommending it. It was the most remarkable victory of the war.

A plaque on Chartres near Conti Street in New Orleans marks the site of Pollock's happiest home. There he brought his bride, Margaret O'Brien, in 1788. There were born their eight children. It was his home when he amassed his great fortune, and continued to be after 1776, when he secretly represented the United States in Spanish New Orleans, fulfilling every request made of him by the Continental Congress, usually also supplying the funds to do it. The Conti Street house was also his office, with his chief clerk, Jean

Anderson, in residence there. He had many plantation properties up the river near Baton Rouge, St. Francisville, and Natchez.

Having spent all his fortune and pledged all his properties in support of the American cause, Pollock was penniless after the war. It was then he moved to Pennsylvania, where he still had a plantation not yet seized by creditors. He spent much of his time trying to get Congress to repay some of his funds, even just the interest, to support his family. Soon after his wife died in 1799, he moved to his daughter's plantation in Pinckneyville, Mississippi. There he lived to see what he had so long advocated—the acquisition of Louisiana and Florida by the United States. He died December 17, 1823. Since 1977 a Mississippi State Archives bronze plaque has marked his grave.

It has been said before, but bears repeating, that the puzzle of Oliver Pollock's long obscurity and neglect by the nation he loved so well is best explained by Pollock himself, who said: "I dwelt in an obscure corner of the Universe, alone and unsupported. I have labored without ceasing; I have neglected the road to affluence, I have exhausted my all and plunged myself deeply into debt to support the cause of America in the hours of her distress . . . [and] I have the heart still ready—had I the means—to bear more suffering and make new sacrifices."

An American like that should not remain forgotten.

J.C.C.

11.

⚜ LOUISIANA PURCHASE ⚜

The Louisiana Purchase (1803) was achieved through an incredible series of improbable events. Napoleon, the First Consul of France, sold something he had neither the moral nor the legal right to sell. The United States ministers, Robert R. Livingston and James Monroe, bought something they were not authorized to buy, and spent seven and a half times the amount of money they were authorized to spend for something else. President Thomas Jefferson, after the Louisiana Purchase, did not believe he had the right under the Constitution of the United States to receive what he had bought. And two British banking houses—Baring and Company and its Amsterdam affiliate, Hope and Company—bought the American stock, issued to pay Napoleon, who used the ready funds to continue the war with England.

The story of the Louisiana Purchase begins in the 1780s, when American farmers in the Ohio Valley first floated their surplus produce in flatboats down the Mississippi to Spanish New Orleans. It was easier for them to get their goods to the eastern American markets by transshipping them from New Orleans than it was to penetrate the trackless wilderness of the Alleghenies.

At first, the Spanish authorities at New Orleans imposed no duties on the American goods but as time passed, and more and more flatboats tied up at the New Orleans levee, the situation changed. Duty was imposed on the American goods, and this was intolerable to the Ohio Valley people. Indignation over the Spanish action expressed itself in several ways. Hotheaded Kentuckians clamored for the raising of a force to descend the Mississippi and seize New Orleans; others demanded that the federal government take either military or diplomatic steps to open the port of New Orleans; yet another element urged that Kentucky secede from the Union and ally itself with Spain so that, as Spanish citizens, they could use the port of New Orleans without paying duty on the deposited goods.

The clamor for the "right of deposit" finally stirred the federal government to action. The American minister to Great Britain, Thomas Pinckney, was dispatched to Spain to seek a treaty which would obtain for the Kentuckians and other Ohio Valley people this right of deposit. In 1795, Pinckney negotiated the Treaty of San Lorenzo—signed at San Lorenzo del Escorial, near Madrid—which gave Americans the right to deposit their goods on the New Orleans levee for three years.

When the treaty expired, the Spanish authorities chose to ignore the fact and the upriver flatboats and keelboats continued to unload their cargoes at New Orleans, unharassed by Spanish tax collectors. Meanwhile, events in Europe were happening fast. Napoleon Bonaparte, First Consul of France—there were three consuls, but the other two were mere rubber stamps, while Napoleon ran the show—persuaded Spain to retrocede Louisiana to France. He promised, in exchange for Louisiana, to place a Spanish prince on the throne of Etruria in Italy and to secure recognition for the new kingdom from England and Russia. Napoleon further pledged that if France did not settle Louisiana, France would not dispose of it to a third party, but would return it to Spain.

When word of the secret Treaty of San Ildefonso, signed on October 1, 1800, leaked out, President Thomas Jefferson was gravely concerned. He loathed Bonaparte and feared France as a neighbor on the western frontier of the United States and especially as the possessor of New Orleans. President Jefferson sent his oft-quoted dispatch to Robert R. Livingston, American minister in Paris: "There is on the globe one single spot, the possessor of which

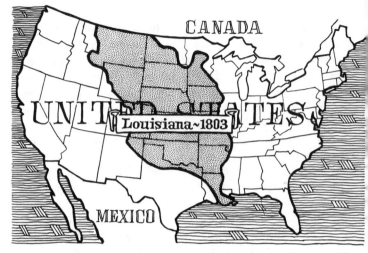

The extraordinary transaction of the Louisiana Purchase, by which Napoleon sold French territory to the Américan government, was completed on December 20, 1803, when the United States flag was raised in Jackson Square. Map by John C. Chase.

is our natural and habitual enemy. It is New Orleans, through which the produce of three-eighths of our territory must pass to market. . . . The day that France takes possession of New Orleans fixes the sentence which is to restrain her forever within her low-water mark. . . . From that moment, we must marry ourselves to the British fleet and nation."

Naturally, Livingston sought all the information he could obtain from the French government, but that master of duplicity, Talleyrand, gave him a superlative demonstration of what a much later generation of Americans would call the "brush off" or the "run-around." After weeks of fruitless effort, Livingston complained to Secretary of State James Madison: "The Minister will give no answer to any inquiries I make on the subject. He will not say what their boundaries are, what are their intentions, and when they are to take possession."

The weeks slipped into months and still Livingston got nowhere. His request that France set a price for New Orleans was ignored. His exasperation was well expressed when he reported on

September 1, 1803: "There never was a government in which less could be done by negotiations than here. There is no people, no legislature, no counsellors. One man is everything. He seldom asks advice and never hears it unasked. His ministers are mere clerks; and his legislature and counsellors parade officers." But even at the height of his frustration, Livingston added a prophetic line: "I am persuaded that the whole [affair] will end in relinquishment of the country and transfer of the capital to the United States."

Up to this point, President Jefferson's motivation was his distaste for Napoleon Bonaparte and the unpalatable fact that France would be our neighbor on the Mississippi. And then a crisis suddenly developed on October 16, 1802, when the Spanish authorities at New Orleans withdrew the right of deposit, which the Americans had continued to exercise even after the Treaty of San Lorenzo had expired.

Was this action inspired by Bonaparte or was it ordered by the Spanish Crown? Or did the Spanish officials at New Orleans act on their own initiative? The Americans in the Ohio Valley, exploding with indignation, didn't care who had denied them the right to get their surplus goods to market through New Orleans. But they did care mightily about using that port. The furor in the Ohio Valley reached Washington, and President Jefferson was more determined than before to acquire New Orleans from France.

It was Napoleon's plan to take possession of Louisiana early in 1803, and he dispatched Pierre Clément de Laussat to New Orleans to make preparations for the arrival of French troops, some of which were to come from Santo Domingo and others to sail from Belgian and Dutch ports. But the Santo Domingo army was virtually wiped out by the rebellious native forces and the yellow fever mosquito. And the ports in the Low Countries became ice-bound, keeping the Louisiana expedition from sailing. With no occupying troops now available, Napoleon began to have second thoughts about Louisiana. He knew that when the war with England broke out again—the Treaty of Amiens was little more than a truce—France could not defend Louisiana. The First Consul decided to sell not just New Orleans but Louisiana to the Americans.

Meanwhile, almost daily, Livingston, in vain, sought a response to his proposal that France sell New Orleans to the United States. To his great surprise one day, Talleyrand replied: "Would you wish to have the whole of Louisiana?" And with that the machinery was set into motion which would, on April 30, 1803, make the vast mid-continental area called Louisiana American. James Monroe joined Livingston in Paris and together they negotiated the Louisiana Purchase Treaty with Napoleon's minister of the treasury.

Napoleon had thus broken his pledge to Spain not to dispose of Louisiana. At the same time, he ignored the French Constitution, under which he was theoretically functioning. This prohibited the disposal of French territory without the approval of the two legislative chambers. So it was that Napoleon had neither the moral nor the legal right to sell Louisiana.

Livingston and Monroe were authorized to spend $2,000,000 for New Orleans. When they agreed to pay $15,000,000, for all of Louisiana, they exceeded their authority seven and a half times.

Thomas Jefferson's "strict construction" view of the Constitution of the United States loomed as an obstacle to his acceptance of Louisiana, once it had been bought. Jefferson's political creed called for the president to construe the Constitution with rigid strictness. If the Constitution didn't spell out what the chief executive should do, he couldn't do it. Jefferson's Federalist opponents held that, by the very nature of the office, the president had broad powers that did not need spelling out. In conformity with his philosophy, Jefferson decided that he needed an amendment to the Constitution to receive Louisiana, and he sat down at his desk and wrote one out.

Fortunately, Jefferson's advisors talked him out of it, pointing out that by the time an amendment went through both houses of Congress and was passed on to the states for ratification, Bonaparte might change his mind and call off the sale of Louisiana. Accordingly, Jefferson put aside for the moment his ideas of strict construction and adopted the Federalists' philosophy of broad, implied powers, to receive Louisiana. In Congress, and in the Federalist press, Jefferson's opponents virtually adopted the president's philosophy to attack him and the Louisiana Purchase.

Facing historic Jackson Square at Chartres and St. Peter streets, the Cabildo was built in 1795 and was the Spanish seat of government. It was here (*in the room upper left*) that the Louisiana Purchase transfer took place. Now fully restored, this magnificent structure is part of the Louisiana State Museum and houses exhibits of historical documents, relics, and mementos of famous New Orleanians. Photo by A. J. Meek.

Napoleon needed money for the resumption of the war with England. Unless he could turn the American stock into ready cash he would be sorely pressed financially. The British banking house of Baring and Company and its Amsterdam affiliate, Hope and Company, came to his rescue. They agreed to buy the stock at 18 percent discount, thus providing Napoleon with the funds to fight their country.

While all this was going on, Laussat dreamed of a new French empire in the New World, with himself playing a significant role in the capital city of New Orleans. Poor Laussat! Napoleon seems to have forgotten about him, and Laussat learned of the sale of Louisiana from American sources. He promptly labeled the news an "incredible and impudent falsehood." But shortly after that, official confirmation arrived from France.

Some historians have pointed out that if Laussat's dream had come true, America might well have been divided into three entities, with the French holding the Mississippi Valley or midsection, the Spanish the western section, and of course the fledgling United States the original thirteen colonies to the east.

This was not to be, however, because on November 30, 1803, in what is now Jackson Square, the Spanish flag came down the flagpole and the Tricolor of Republican France went up. For twenty days, Laussat administered Louisiana for France, and then, on December 20, the French standard gave way to the American flag and Louisiana became a territory of the United States.

C.L.D.

BIBLIOGRAPHY

Chase, John C. *The Louisiana Purchase.* 2nd ed. New Orleans, 1982.
Dufour, Charles L. *Ten Flags in the Wind.* New York, 1967.

12.

 BATTLE OF NEW ORLEANS

Six miles down the Mississippi River from the Vieux Carré lie the plains of Chalmette, where Andrew Jackson's ragtag American army defeated the British in the Battle of New Orleans on January 8, 1815. This engagement, when the Americans behind their mud ramparts repulsed the attack of General Edward Pakenham's crack army, fresh from victories in Spain, was the culminating action in the British campaign for New Orleans.

The British opened a five-phase operation by capturing five American gunboats on Lake Borgne in an unequal engagement on December 14, 1814. None of the American sailors escaped capture, so no word of the British troop movements reached New Orleans. General Jackson was completely in the dark as to the whereabouts of the British until December 23. On that day, advance elements of Pakenham's army reached the Villeré plantation, capturing a token force under young Major Gabriel Villeré. The latter managed to escape to bring the news to Jackson about noon. "By the Eternal, they shall not sleep on our soil," he thundered. He immediately called in his troops from various outlying areas and prepared to attack the British camp that very night.

At 7:30 P.M., as the American gunboat *Carolina* began lobbing shells into the British position, Jackson struck. In the darkness the fighting was confused and indecisive, although both sides afterwards claimed victory. Jackson disengaged his troops and fell back to the Rodriguez Canal, an abandoned millrace. Jackson's men, working all night, deepened the canal and threw up breastworks behind it. Interestingly, about the very time in the early hours of Christmas Eve that Jackson was digging in, American and British peace commissioners, far away in Ghent, Belgium, were preparing to sign the peace treaty.

Jackson's fortified line ran from the Mississippi to the swamp, a distance of about three-quarters of a mile. But Jackson failed to make his extreme left secure and his line was exposed at that point. Pakenham launched, on December 28, a reconnaissance in force to probe the American position, and British troops on Pakenham's extreme right actually outflanked the exposed American left. Disaster for Jackson was averted, when the British commander, ill-informed on the progress along the entire front, and thus ignorant of the success on his right, ordered a general retirement. The well-disciplined British soldiers who had turned Jackson's exposed left, obeyed the recall signal of the bugles and could not exploit their success. Jackson immediately reinforced his left, bending his line deep into the swamp, thus making it virtually impossible for the British again to turn it.

The fourth engagement of the British campaign for New Orleans was an artillery duel on January 1, 1815. After an extended exchange of effective fire, the American gunners—including two of Jean Laffite's Baratarians, Dominique You and René Beluche—succeeded in silencing the British batteries. It is legendary that on January 8 the Americans fought behind cotton bales. But as with so many legends, this is not true. Indeed, cotton bales were originally implanted in the mud ramparts behind the Rodriguez Canal, but the British cannonade on New Year's Day knocked the bales out of the line and set some on fire. Jackson ordered the bales removed. So when Pakenham made his grand assault, on January 8, there were no cotton bales in the American line.

For this major effort against the American position, Pakenham planned well. He would send fourteen hundred troops across the river to attack Jackson's West Bank line in coordination with the major assault against the American breastworks at Chalmette.

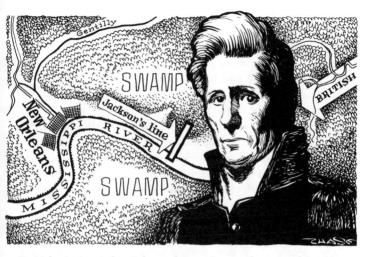

By this battle plan, Andrew Jackson and his small, ragtag force successfully withstood the British advance in the Battle of New Orleans, 1815. A representation of the battle and a restoration of General Jackson's line can be seen in the Chalmette National Park, actual site of the fighting. Illustration by John C. Chase.

Once the West Bank line was carried, the American guns were to be turned against the American line at Chalmette. Thus Jackson would be fixed by both enfilading and frontal fire and his position would be precarious, if not untenable. Had the execution been as good as the conception, Jackson in all probability would have had to pull out of the Chalmette fortification and establish a new line closer to the city. But several things went wrong. A canal, hastily improvised to get small boats into the river, proved inadequate and only six hundred troops, not fourteen hundred, actually reached the West Bank, after a considerable delay. Then the river's swift current carried the boats downstream a good distance from the designated line of departure. Accordingly, when Pakenham opened the battle at Chalmette at sunrise on January 8, his West Bank force was far from ready to attack.

As the British moved on Jackson's line they were met by what one of Pakenham's officers called "the most murderous and destructive fire of all arms ever poured upon a column." Pakenham, as he spurred his horse past General John Lambert, shouted: "That's a terrific fire, Lambert." Moments later his horse was shot from under him, and a bullet shattered one of his knees. The gallant British commander mounted another horse, but as he settled in the saddle and gave it spur, another bullet struck him in the spine. He was carried, dying, from the field.

Shortly after Pakenham fell, General Samuel Gibbs was mortally wounded and General John Keane was severely struck and was forced from the field. The British command now fell to General Lambert, who tried in vain to re-form his shattered regiments, melting away under the withering American fire. He sought a truce from Jackson, which the latter readily agreed to, and promptly recalled the British force from the West Bank.

The British had waged a successful attack on the West Bank, but it was a belated one due to the delays in getting it under way. Accordingly, by the time the American line had been captured, the battle at Chalmette had been lost, with frightful casualties in officers and men. "The whole plain on the left, as also the side by the river . . . was covered with the British soldiers who had fallen," wrote one of Jackson's officers. American losses on January 8 were 7 killed and 6 wounded. For the entire five-phase campaign, American losses were 333 killed, wounded, and missing. The British casualties were 393 dead, 1,514 wounded, and 522 missing.

For ten days, the British ostensibly occupied their lines at Chalmette, but actually General Lambert had begun moving his troops out in the quiet of night. The sound of drums and bugles by day and the continuing glow of campfires by night served to cover the British evacuation. On the morning of January 19 a flock of buzzards hovered over the British camp, suggesting that something was amiss. Jackson sent scouts to investigate and they reported that the camp was deserted. The last of the invading army had slipped away. On the same day, seventy-five miles below New Orleans, two British bomb boats gave up their nine-day futile efforts to silence the guns of Fort St. Philip.

Romancers and movie-makers have glamorized the part that

Andrew Jackson defeats the British army under the command of Sir Edward Pakenham, January 8, 1815. The Historic New Orleans Collection.

Jean Laffite and the Baratarian pirates played in the American victory. Neither Jean, nor his brother Pierre, was on the battlefield on January 8. Their greatest contribution was in supplying the Americans with flints for their muskets and making the expert artillerists, You and Beluche, available to Jackson.

Although fought two weeks after the Treaty of Ghent had been signed, the Battle of New Orleans was significant for several reasons. It marked the last shedding of blood between the two great

English-speaking nations; the eight thousand troops that withdrew from Chalmette joined the Duke of Wellington in Belgium in time for the Battle of Waterloo; Jackson's victory ultimately sent him to the White House.

The Chalmette Battlefield Park on Louisiana Highway 46, six miles from the Vieux Carré, is reached from St. Claude Avenue. The National Park Service Visitor Center provides interpretive exhibits and a slide description of the British campaign. Jackson's Rodriguez Canal line has been restored and one may follow a self-guided tour of the battlefield.

C.L.D.

BIBLIOGRAPHY

Dufour, Charles L. *Ten Flags in the Wind*. New York, 1967.

13.

❧ THE CIVIL WAR ❧

In the spring of 1860, when the political pot began to bubble, the state of Louisiana had no grievance against the Federal government. Indeed, there was no reason for one. Louisiana's sugar industry was protected by a tariff. The port of New Orleans, the world's greatest export port at the time, was booming, with receipts of more than $185 million. Its banking system—thirteen New Orleans banks had deposits of almost $20 million and gold specie of more than $12 million—was the soundest in the nation. And Louisiana's per capita wealth placed it second only to tiny Connecticut.

Even when the presidential election came, despite months of political tension leading up to it, Union sentiment in Louisiana outweighed secession opinion. This is reflected in the election returns in November, 1860, when a majority of the 50,000 who went to the polls voted for pro-Union candidates John Bell (20,204) and Stephen A. Douglas (7,625) for a majority of 5,148 over the secession candidate, John C. Breckinridge (22,681). Abraham Lincoln's name was not on the ballot in Louisiana.

The election of Lincoln set the machinery of secession into motion throughout the South. Louisiana was no exception, although voices of moderation were not stilled by the clamor for disunion. The *True Delta* reflected Union sentiment in New Orleans: "Lincoln cannot, however disposed himself . . . do aught against the rights of any section of the Union. . . . Why then, under such circumstances should Louisiana countenance designs against the Union?" The *Bee*, which reminded its readers that it had been "uniformly attached to the Union," declared: "It will be time to fight Lincoln with gunpowder and sword when we find either that constitutional resistance fails, or that he and his party are bent on our humiliation and destruction."

But in a matter of weeks sentiment changed. The *Bee*, in December, clamored for secession. A northerner residing in New Orleans confided to his diary: "I am myself drifting into secession ideas." And William A. Mure, British consul, reported to the Foreign Office that when he returned to New Orleans from leave, he was astonished "to find the feeling in favour of Secession so strong or general as it is in this City and State."

How did such a change of sentiment come about? The pulpit oratory of Dr. Benjamin M. Palmer, New Orleans' most eloquent preacher, was the principal factor that swung opinion to secession. On Thanksgiving Day, Dr. Palmer mounted the pulpit of the First Presbyterian Church and for two hours held a capacity audience spellbound as he defended slavery, denounced the "undeniably atheistic" abolitionists, and called upon the people of the South to "reclaim the powers they have delegated." Profoundly impressed, the people left the church. An eyewitness recalled: "After the benediction, in solemn silence, no man speaking to his neighbor, the great congregation of serious and thoughtful men and women dispersed; but afterwards the drums beat and the bugles sounded; for New Orleans was shouting for secession." The evils of slavery became lost in the emotions of the times, and not until the scars of war had begun to heal would New Orleanians realize it.

On January 26, 1861, a convention called to consider Louisiana's relationship to the Union, overwhelmingly passed the Ordinance of Secession by a vote of 113 to 17. Ten days later, six Louisiana delegates to a convention in Montgomery, Alabama, helped to form the Confederate States of America.

Even before Louisiana seceded from the Union, Governor Thomas O. Moore took direct action against the Federal government. He seized Forts Jackson and St. Philip, seventy-five miles downriver from New Orleans, the arsenal in Baton Rouge, and other United States installations in Louisiana. After secession, Governor Moore seized the U.S. Mint and the Custom House.

New Orleans bustled with troops which went into camp, initially, at the Metairie Race Course, renamed Camp Leroy Pope Walker for the Confederate secretary of war. After the firing on Fort Sumter and its fall—Louisiana's P. G. T. Beauregard was the Confederate commander at Charleston—Louisiana troops daily jammed the trains heading for the war zone in Virginia. The war became a reality to New Orleanians on May 26, when the Federal blockade of the mouth of the Mississippi began. As such staples as coffee, flour, and soap became scarce its effectiveness sent prices soaring.

The defense of New Orleans was placed in the hands of General David E. Twiggs, who joined the Confederacy after serving fifty years in the United States Army. But at seventy-one, Twiggs was hardly the man of driving energy that the command post at New Orleans demanded. Finally, in October, Twiggs was replaced by General Mansfield Lovell, who found the situation at New Orleans a chaotic one. With tireless energy—the press described it as "restless activity"—General Lovell bent to the task of preparing New Orleans for the Union attack, the inevitability of which appeared more certain as the weeks went by.

Lovell's tremendous task was not made any easier by the Rich-mond government's inability to realize the imminent danger of a naval attack on New Orleans, or by the Confederate navy's stub-born resistance to a coordinated defense plan. As he pushed forward with his preparations Lovell nevertheless found several things to please him. The *Manassas*, the Civil War's first ironclad, had driven a Union flotilla out of the river in a night engagement at the Head of the Passes (mouth of the Mississippi). Two giant ironclads, the *Mississippi* and the *Louisiana*, were on the ways and their builders assured Lovell that the ships would be ready for action by the end of January. Each was to have great firepower, and armor plate would render them impervious to normal shot and shell. But delay upon delay slowed construction of these two mightiest warships in the world, and they were still far from ready for action when Captain David G. Farragut launched his attack on Forts Jackson and St. Philip, which if successful would ensure the capture of New Orleans.

Fate conspired against the Confederacy at New Orleans, for the barrier which Lovell had constructed in the river between the two forts was swept away by unduly high water and the debris that accumulated behind it. Lovell had a new barrier improvised, but it was by no means impregnable, particularly because the Confederate navy failed to patrol it effectively.

Although Farragut had reached Ship Island as early as February 20, it was not until April 8 that he had his fleet of seventeen warships (all wooden vessels) and twenty mortar boats safely in the river at the Head of the Passes. On April 18 the mortar boats, under Commander David Dixon Porter, opened fire on the forts. Incessantly, for five days and nights, Porter's mortars lobbed shells into the Confederate forts. Although the fire was "accurate and terrible," as Confederate General J. K. Duncan put it, the Confederate batteries were not silenced and continued their heavy response. Then it was that Farragut, certain that Porter's flotilla could not neutralize the Confederate forts, decided to make the run past them.

An expedition was sent out to inspect the improvised barrier, which Lovell hoped would hold the Union fleet under the fire of the forts. The party returned to Farragut with word that it had been able, unchallenged, to cut an opening in the barrier through which the attacking vessels could pass. Farragut then set 2:00 A.M. on April 24 as the time for the hazardous operation to begin.

At 3:30 A.M., the *Cayuga*, Farragut's lead vessel, slipped almost noiselessly through the opening in the barrier, holding its fire. Alert lookouts in Fort Jackson spotted the "black, shapeless masses . . . moving silently up the river," and the fort's guns blazed away. At the sound of the guns, six vessels in the so-called River Defense Fleet fled ingloriously from the scene, but three other Confederate vessels, *Manassas*, *McRae*, and *Governor Moore*, fought with spectacular valor. The moonless night was brightly lit by the flashing guns and the bursting shells during the furious duel. A Union officer described the awesome scene: "Combine all that you have heard of thunder, add to it all that you have seen of lightning, and you have, perhaps, a conception of the scene." Another Union officer described it as "the breaking up of the universe with the moon and all the stars bursting in our midst." Farragut himself said "it was as if the artillery of heaven were playing upon the earth."

Farragut's flagship *Hartford*, during the height of the fighting, ran aground and was set ablaze when it was rammed by a Confederate fire raft. But the *Hartford* broke free of the sandbar and steamed past the forts to safety. Fourteen of the seventeen Union warships successfully ran the fiery gantlet.

The performance of the Confederate *Governor Moore* during the battle was one of the Civil War's great feats of valor. Alone, after the *Manassas* and the *McRae* were disabled, the former scuttled, the latter with its steering gear shot away, the *Governor Moore* took on the whole Union fleet, before engaging the *Varuna* in a running battle. This ended when the *Governor Moore* sank the *Varuna* by ramming it, after which its valiant commander, Lieutenant Beverly Kennon, set his shattered vessel afire and threw his sword into the river before surrendering. The toll of fifty-seven dead aboard the *Governor Moore* was greater than the total killed in the two Confederate forts and Farragut's entire fleet.

New Orleans was panic-stricken when the news arrived that the Union fleet had passed the forts and was steaming upstream to the city. Lovell removed his wholly inadequate militia force from the city. Warehouses were emptied of cotton, sugar, rice, and corn, which were brought in drays to the levee and set on fire. The *Mississippi*, far from completed, was fired and set adrift in the river. Down at the forts, which surrendered to Commander Porter following a mutiny, the *Louisiana* was blown up by its crew. The *Louisiana*, lacking motive power, had been towed to Fort St. Philip to be used as a floating battery, but it played no part in the battle.

On April 25, Farragut's fleet dropped anchor before New Orleans. After four days of acrimonious correspondence between the Union commander and Mayor John T. Monroe, Farragut sent a

In April, 1862, Admiral Farragut's fleet of fourteen Union warships, shown off Canal Street, successfully ran past Forts Jackson and St. Philip to reach New Orleans. This marked the end of the city as a Confederate stronghold. On May 1

General Benjamin Butler arrived and military rule was imposed. The Historic New Orleans Collection.

detachment ashore to raise the American flag over City Hall. It was the end of Confederate New Orleans. The occupying army of General Benjamin F. Butler disembarked on May 1 and the dark days of Reconstruction began. Butler's rule was a tempestuous one and he soon was loathed in New Orleans, thoroughly hated in the South, looked upon with suspicion in the North, and denounced in the British Parliament.

One may question whether Butler really deserved the name "Spoons," because of his alleged predilection for other people's table silver, or "Beast," because he outraged the sensibilities of the people of New Orleans by what was universally called the "infamous woman order." When the women of New Orleans, even the fashionable ladies of the city, emphasized their scorn for the occupying troops by spitting on them or deluging passing soldiers from balconies, Butler issued General Order No. 28. This ordered "that hereafter when any female shall, by word, gesture, or movement, insult or show contempt for any officer of the United States, she shall be regarded and held liable to be treated as a woman of the town plying her avocation."

For fifteen years, Federal troops supported carpetbag regimes in Louisiana, from 1862 to 1877. These were years of arrogant misgovernment, unashamed graft, rampant corruption, and open thievery in law-making and law-enforcing bodies.

The end finally came after the disputed election of 1876 in which Rutherford B. Hayes was awarded the presidency over Samuel J. Tilden by one electoral vote, when Louisiana's fraudulent electoral vote was counted for Hayes. At the same election, Louisiana emerged with two governors, the Republican carpetbagger, Stephen B. Packard, and former Confederate General Francis T. Nicholls, who had lost a foot and an arm in the Civil War.

A deal was made with Hayes's managers whereby the new president would withdraw the Federal troops which supported Packard's regime in return for which Nicholls would not contest the state's electoral vote going to Hayes. On April 24, 1877, President Hayes ordered all Federal troops out of New Orleans. With this support gone, the Packard regime collapsed, leaving Governor Nicholls as the legal chief executive of Louisiana. Reconstruction,

TO THE PEOPLE

OF

NEW ORLEANS.

Mayoralty of New Orleans,

CITY HALL, April 25th, 1862.

After an obstinate and heroic defence by our troops on the river, there appears to be imminent danger that the insolent enemy will succeed in capturing your city. The forts have not fallen; they have not succumbed even beneath the terrors of a bombardment unparalleled in the history of warfare. Their defenders have done all that becomes men fighting for their homes, their country and their liberty; but in spite of their efforts, the ships of the enemy have been able to avoid them, and now threaten the city. In view of this contingency, I call on you to be calm, to meet the enemy, not with submissiveness nor with indecent alacrity; but if the military authorities are unable longer to defend you, to await with hope and confidence the inevitable moment when the valor of your sons and of your fellow-countrymen will achieve your deliverance. I shall remain among you, to protect you and your property, so far as my power or authority as Chief Magistrate can avail.

JOHN T. MONROE,

MAYOR.

Mayor Monroe's proclamation, 1862. The Historic New Orleans Collection.

with all its corruption and frustrations, was over and at long last home rule was restored to Louisiana.

C.L.D.

BIBLIOGRAPHY

Dufour, Charles L. *The Night the War Was Lost*. Garden City, 1960.

14.

 RECONSTRUCTION AND AFTER

The shooting did not start in New Orleans until after the Civil War was over. Once the South's surrender came, it ushered in a bloody period of riots, political chaos, tense confrontations, and decisions that affected the course of the nation's history. Negotiations masterminded from the city made a president of the United States. The separate but equal doctrine that governed American race relations for more than the first half of the twentieth century developed out of a New Orleans challenge. Once, two rival state governments tried to rule at the same time.

The Union soldiers of General Benjamin F. Butler occupied the city in 1862 without firing a rifle because the fate of New Orleans had been decided when David Farragut's fleet steamed past the downriver forts. Federal units maintained a military presence until the spring of 1877. Their bayonets cast a shadow over the city throughout the era of Reconstruction.

As the then capital of Louisiana, New Orleans was the focal point of the struggle between the Radical Republicans and the Conservative Democrats. On the Republican side were the carpetbaggers and scalawags who sought to entrench themselves in power through their appeal to freed slaves and other Negroes. On the Democratic side were the Louisianians who had fought for or sympathized with the Confederacy and still were willing to risk their lives in order to maintain white supremacy. As long as they had the support of Federal troops, the Republicans held the trappings of power. Once the soldiers marched away, the Democrats took control.

Michael Hahn, who became governor in the closing months of the war, and Henry Clay Warmoth, elected in 1868, conducted Republican administrations without direct competition from Democratic challengers. The awkward situation of dual governments began with the disputed election of 1872. Both parties claimed victory. The Republicans owned the counting apparatus, and could hardly lose. Out in the country parishes, the night-riding planters, all Democrats, killed and bulldozed to keep Negroes from the polls and thus reduce Republican totals.

William Pitt Kellogg, Republican, took the oath as governor on January 13, 1873, in the Mechanics' Institute, then the statehouse, while on the same day the Democrats inaugurated John McEnery in ceremonies in Lafayette Square. Rival legislatures were convened. Kellogg prevailed for four years because he had the support of President Ulysses S. Grant, but the effectiveness of his regime was largely nullified by insurrection in 1874 culminating in a battle in the French Quarter involving more than ten thousand men.

The national political climate had changed by the time of the election of 1876 in which Louisianians voted for a president and a governor. Citizens in the North had grown tired of seeing carpetbag regimes in the South clinging to office only because Federal troops were on hand. The resurgent national Democratic party nominated Samuel J. Tilden for president, while the Republicans picked Rutherford B. Hayes. For governor, Louisiana Democrats chose Francis T. Nicholls, a former Confederate general, and the Republicans settled on Stephen B. Packard, the United States marshal.

Again the night-riders ranged through rural Louisiana, and again the Republican counting board threw out enough Democratic ballots to give undisputed majorities to Hayes and Packard. As controversy over the returns raged, Louisiana's electoral vote became pivotal in the presidential race. The election was contested

Two governors were inaugurated on the same day in 1877—Stephen B. Packard (Republican) and Francis T. Nicholls (Democrat). Ultimately Nicholls was recognized as the legitimate governor. The Historic New Orleans Collection.

not only in Louisiana but also in South Carolina and Florida, the other states where United States soldiers still were stationed. If Hayes were awarded all of the electoral votes from the three states, he would win by one vote. If Tilden were given only one of the states, he would have the electoral votes to be elected.

A complicated situation, unforeseen by the framers of the Constitution, resulted when two sets of electoral returns reached the president of the Senate. Which legislative body was to count them? If the Republican Senate, the Republican returns would be counted; if the Democratic House, the Democratic returns. To settle this unique stalemate, Congress established a fifteen-man commission, made up of five Republican senators, five House Democrats, and five justices of the Supreme Court. There were two justices from each political party named and they were to pick the fifth. The justices chose David Davis, an independent Republican, but he was elected to the Senate by the Illinois legislature and promptly withdrew from the commission. In his place Justice Joseph P. Bradley, a Republican, was chosen.

Throughout February, the commission deliberated and studied the returns and when, finally, the vote came, it was a strictly partisan division, 8 to 7 in favor of Hayes on every disputed electoral vote. And so Hayes won the presidency, 185 electoral votes to 184, just two days before he was sworn in on March 4, 1877.

Meanwhile, from New Orleans, Nicholls began negotiating with Hayes's faction through intermediaries in Washington. A deal was struck under which the Louisiana Democratic party would accept the decision without opposition provided that Hayes agree to recognize Nicholls' Democratic government in Louisiana and to pull out the Federal troops, thus ending Reconstruction.

For weeks Nicholls and Packard each had attempted to run the state. Nicholls' legislature met in the Odd Fellows Hall, while Packard and his legislators tried to do business in the St. Louis Hotel under the protection of the Metropolitan Police. The hotel, which stood on St. Louis Street where the Royal Orleans Hotel now is situated, had been purchased for use as the statehouse by the

Kellogg administration. A contingent of United States soldiers was quartered in an adjacent hotel. On April 24, 1877, Hayes lived up to his word. He sent the troops away in a symbolic admission that home rule had been restored in Louisiana. Packard's administration collapsed, leaving Nicholls and the Democrats in full control.

The firing of a one-hundred-gun salute on the riverbank at Canal Street was a thunderous finale to fifteen years of conflict that began with the Union occupation in 1862. In that period politics had been a deadly business. On one side were men who wanted to help former slaves enjoy some of the rewards of freedom, along with ambitious newcomers and a few native-born Louisianians who used the Negro as a pawn to win selfish advantages. On the other side were the uncompromising conservatives who felt that the uneducated Negroes were not qualified for full citizenship, and who would resist any move toward equality. The issues that divided conservatives and radicals were the kind that cause men to kill each other.

The tense situation exploded on July 30, 1866, around the Mechanics' Institute, which stood on the site now occupied by the Fairmont Hotel. A massacre was touched off by the attempt of some black delegates to reconvene the Louisiana constitutional convention of 1864 with the purpose of giving voting rights to Negroes and taking them away from former Confederate soldiers. Because of a misunderstanding, Federal occupation troops were not on hand to prevent disorder. But Mayor John T. Monroe, who was determined to block the meeting, had a large contingent of city policemen at the scene. A skirmish broke out shortly after noon as a procession of Negroes marched to the hall. The police and an assemblage of whites opened fire, and the Negroes sought refuge in the institute. For two hours the whites poured rifle and pistol fire into the building. A few of the Negroes were armed, and shot at the attackers from the windows. When it became apparent that no surrender would be accepted, Negroes began leaping out of the windows, only to fall into the hands of their foes. The belated arrival of United States soldiers finally halted the slaughter.

THE LOUISIANA OUTRAGES—ATTACK UPON THE POLICE IN THE STREETS OF NEW ORLEANS.

The Battle of Liberty Place, 1874, between the White League and the Metropolitan Police occurred on September 14. Here the White League's attack was in front of the Custom House on Canal Street. The Historic New Orleans Collection.

Thirty-four Negroes and 3 whites in the beleaguered convention group were killed, and 119 Negroes and 17 whites wounded. Ten policemen were injured and one of the attacking whites was fatally wounded. The former governor, Michael Hahn, was among those hurt.

The massacre was among the earliest and bloodiest of the deadly incidents of the Reconstruction period in Louisiana. The hatreds that culminated in the war were by no means appeased by the surrender.

The attempt of the Radical Republicans to govern the state was not peaceably accepted in the rural areas any more than it was in New Orleans. On Easter Day, 1873, a battle was fought at Colfax between Negroes who had armed themselves and taken over the town, and whites, many of them former Confederate soldiers. Thirty-seven Negroes who were taken prisoner in an assault on the courthouse where they had barricaded themselves were ushered out and shot down. When Federal authorities finally arrived they found sixty-nine Negroes dead.

The climax to Reconstruction in New Orleans came on September 14, 1874, although there would be two and a half more years of strife. New Orleanians know the big event as the Battle of Liberty Place or the Battle of September Fourteenth. Battle is no exaggerated description of the showdown between the carpetbag government and the White League. Historian Joe Gray Taylor estimates that on one side were 500 members of the Metropolitan Police, 100 additional police officers, and a militia force of about 3,000 Negroes. On the other were about 8,400 men. There had been full-blown confrontations during the recent war in which the opposing forces were no greater. Ironically, the commander of the carpetbag troops was James Longstreet, perhaps Robert E. Lee's favorite among his Confederate generals. Longstreet had become a Republican. The leader of the White League, the First Louisiana Regiment, and other volunteers was Frederick N. Ogden, a highly respected resident who had been a Confederate major.

The showdown was precipitated by the arrival of the steamer *Mississippi* with a cargo of arms intended for the rebellious Conservative Democrats. Governor Kellogg's Metropolitan Police were ordered to keep the weapons from being distributed; the Democrats were determined to take advantage of them. Public sentiment was whipped up at a mass meeting held that Monday morning around the statue of Henry Clay that stood at the intersection of Canal and St. Charles streets. Meanwhile, Ogden deployed his forces. Streetcars were overturned to provide barricades at intersections along Poydras Street. This established a line of defense in case a retreat became necessary.

By afternoon the two armies faced each other along a front that stretched from the river to the Custom House on Canal Street. Both sides had artillery pieces, although few if any shells were fired once the action began. Ogden's men charged, routing the Metropolitan Police, with the result that the militia retreated. Some of the police troopers dived into the river in their effort to get away from their pursuers. A young boy who grew up to be one of New Orleans' ablest mayors, Martin Behrman, picked up in the French Quarter a rifle that he saw ditched by a fleeing trooper. Many hundreds of spectators had a closeup view of the action. Some lined up on Canal Street. Others stood at the rails of two steamboats moored near the foot of Canal Street.

The issue was settled so quickly that there were few casualties. Longstreet lost eleven men and Ogden twenty-one. The Democrats had the upper hand for two days, but more Union troops were sent into the city, and the Kellogg administration regained control.

The departure of Federal troops brought no lasting peace to nineteenth-century New Orleans. The violence and contempt for authority that accompanied Reconstruction left hangovers that persisted for years. Gunslingers of the Wild West had their counterparts in the big port on the Mississippi River. A sizable segment of the male population, rich or poor, routinely stuffed pistols into pockets when leaving home. Weapons were hair-triggered, and so were the tempers of their owners.

Gradually home rule was reestablished by the Democrats who took over control of state and local government. Then a new irritant developed with the wholesale influx of Italians seeking escape from the hopeless poverty of their native island of Sicily. Most were unskilled and uneducated, no economic assets to a community which already had an oversupply of black day-laborers. Hundreds of the newcomers settled into a ghetto in the French Quarter. A part of Decatur Street was known as Vendetta Alley because many of the immigrants brought their knives along, and sometimes used them. Crimes, mostly against Italians, were charged to the Black Hand or Mafia. Whether, as some authorities have contended, the Mafia was introduced in New Orleans is an unsettled question. At any rate, the white establishment that had finally prevailed over Negroes and carpetbaggers made no attempt to conceal its hostility to the newcomers.

When an Italian family that supplied stevedores on the

riverfront ambushed a rival family in 1890, Police Superintendent David C. Hennessy warned that he would not tolerate gang warfare. On the night of October 15, 1890, Hennessy was waylaid and mowed down with shotgun fire outside his home, near what is now the site of the Louisiana Superdome. When asked who shot him, he whispered, "Dagoes." He died without giving any details. Mayor Joseph Shakspeare ordered police to round up every Italian they could find in the area.

Nineteen Sicilians were indicted and nine went on trial. There was no doubt about the sentiments of many New Orleanians. A crowd gathered outside the courthouse every morning and taunted the defendants as they were brought from the prison. "Who killa da chief?" was the shout, and it became a catchphrase in New Orleans. Testimony was equivocal, at best, but newspaper accounts of the trial made it appear that the eight men and a boy had been proven guilty. As a result, there was a jolt when the jury found six defendants innocent, and said it could not agree on a verdict so far as the other three were concerned. The Italians were taken back to the parish prison because other charges were pending.

The morning newspapers of March 14, 1891, printed an announcement signed by sixty-one citizens calling for a mass meeting on Canal Street at the Clay statue at ten o'clock to consider what to do about the verdict. The *Daily States* published a page-one editorial calling for the people to take the law into their own hands. Hundreds heard inflammatory speeches, then started streaming toward the parish prison, which stood on a square now occupied by a pumping station behind the Municipal Auditorium and alongside the Theater of the Performing Arts. The mob used a battering ram to force its way into the prison. Nine Italians were shot to death inside, and two others were dragged outside and hanged, to appease the appetite of thousands who were shouting for blood.

An international uproar ensued. The United States government paid an indemnity of $24,330 to the Italian government. Some New Orleanians feared that the Italian navy would steam up the Mississippi River and shell the city.

Once President Hayes withdrew the United States soldiers, the white Democrats went about the business of taking away most of the privileges won for Negroes in the Civil War. By the beginning of the twentieth century Negroes had been effectively disfranchised, and even before that they had been driven from public schools and public accommodations. Act III adopted by the Louisiana Legislature in 1890 provided for separation of the races in public vehicles.

Members of the Comité des Citoyens, many of whom had been free men of color before the war, gagged at this infringement of their rights and fought in the courts. It was a disastrous move for American Negroes. Out of the action begun in New Orleans came the decision of the United States Supreme Court that a policy of providing separate but equal facilities for the races was constitutional. For longer than half a century, until the Court reversed itself in the Topeka school cases in 1954, Negroes in the United States were separate, but far from equal.

For a test case, the Comité chose Homer Adolph Plessy, a shoemaker whose blood was only one-eighth Negro but who by definition of the law was a Negro. His skin was so pale that he could have gone unnoticed in any assembly of Caucasians. But on June 7, 1892, he boarded an East Louisiana Railroad train and took a seat in a car reserved for whites. He made a point of informing the conductor that he was an octoroon, and by prearrangement he was arrested and haled before Judge John H. Ferguson of the state court. The judge found him guilty of violating the law, and the Comité's appeal on behalf of the defendant was the *Plessy* v. *Ferguson* case so widely cited in American jurisprudence. Supreme Court Justice John Marshall Harlan wrote in 1896 that "our constitution is color blind," but the other justices outvoted him, and the precedent was set. Of course, the politics of the times made the decision inevitable, and if it had not come from the case originating in New Orleans it would have resulted sooner or later from a test made somewhere else. Plessy eventually was fined $25.

The only major race riot ever to occur in New Orleans, the murderous Robert Charles outbreak in July, 1900, could be regarded as the final spasm of the violent postwar era. The Mississippi-born Charles was interested in the back-to-Africa movement, but had no reputation as a militant. He had a gunfight with a policeman who sought to question him about sitting on a Dryades Street doorstep late at night, then he killed two officers who went to his residence to question him. Charles hid for three days in a two-story frame annex to a residence at 1208 South Saratoga, in the block bounded by South Rampart, Clio, and Erato. When he was found, he fatally wounded two more policemen, then fought back against a siege by some five thousand men who surrounded the structure. Finally the annex was set afire and Charles was driven out and mowed down. His body was riddled with bullets. In all, Charles killed seven men, including the four policemen, seriously wounded seven other persons, and inflicted minor wounds on still another twelve. Marauding mobs roamed the city, killing about a dozen Negroes and injuring many others.

A community's fury was largely spent in the Robert Charles orgy of hatred. There would be disorders during the racial revolution of the 1960s and 1970s, and an ugly incident in 1973, when sniper Mark Essex paralyzed the Central Business District for a night and day. Yet after 1900, relations between the races were more relaxed in New Orleans than they were in any other large southern city. One factor was proximity. Neighborhoods in the older residential districts are checkerboards, and many are fully mixed. Ghettoes did not develop until public housing projects were built during the mid-1930s and afterward and until blacks occupied thousands of houses vacated in the white flight to the suburbs.

As blacks won voting rights and acquired numerical superiority a new era dawned, marked in 1978 by the election and in 1982 by the reelection of the first black mayor, Ernest N. Morial. New Orleanians of Italian heritage had to wait only forty-five years after the lynching: Mayor Robert S. Maestri was inaugurated in 1936. Maestri won the job without an election, but in 1962, Victor H. Schiro proved that old-time prejudices no longer ruled—he was swept into office with a majority vote.

J. W.

BIBLIOGRAPHY

Dufour, Charles L. *Ten Flags in the Wind.* New York, 1967.

Hair, William Ivy. *Carnival of Fury.* Baton Rouge, 1976.

Taylor, Joe Gray. *Louisiana Reconstructed, 1863–1877.* Baton Rouge, 1975.

15.

❧ YELLOW FEVER ❧

The scenes were out of the Dark Ages. Clouds of black smoke rising from barrels of tar set aflame on street corners. The roar of cannon aimed skyward in public squares. The stench of carbolic acid brimming in the gutters. The processions wending their way to the cemeteries.

Throughout the nineteenth century and even into the twentieth, New Orleans periodically was overwhelmed by onslaughts of disease—Asiatic cholera, bubonic plague, and, above all, yellow fever. As in medieval times, medical science could not cope with the emergencies, and the grieving, desperate populace turned to any farfetched measure that had a glimmer of plausibility, even one with overtones of witchcraft. The six-pounders were not actually aimed at evil spirits hovering over the stricken city. There were theories that the concussion of the blasts would break up a death-dealing miasma that had settled overhead, that the tar fires would purify the atmosphere, that fumes from the acid would kill the organisms that were making people sick.

The toll was appalling. An outbreak of Asiatic cholera in 1832 claimed 4,340 lives in a population that started at about 50,000 but had dwindled to no more than 35,000 as every family that could afford to get away fled the city. In 1853, yellow fever invaded in a slaughter that historian John Duffy has described as "probably the worst single epidemic ever to strike a major American city."

The toll was 7,849 lives. In the years between 1793 and 1905, yellow fever caused 100,000 deaths in New Orleans, and almost as many more in the immediate area. The unrecognized enemy in all of the time before the advent of the twentieth century, a menace that seriously threatened to make a world port uninhabitable by humans, was a mosquito, the *Aedes aegypti*, whose bite spread the fever. As recently as 1914 an outbreak of bubonic plague alarmed citizens, although a rat-trapping campaign halted the spread of the disease, and only 10 deaths were recorded.

As terrible as the epidemics were, they only underscored the health problems of a semitropical port into which every arriving ship was the potential carrier of exotic disease. Smallpox, malaria, typhoid, tuberculosis, syphilis, they were almost endemic in an urban area devoid of even the rudiments of sanitation. More than one contemporary writer called New Orleans the filthiest city in the United States. Unpaved streets were lined with open drainage ditches, which stank from an accumulation of human excrement, dead animals, and kitchen slops. Lumbering wagons collected the night soil from outdoor privies and hauled it to a nuisance wharf, where it was transferred to barges and dumped into the Mississippi River. Often the barge operators discharged their cargoes where steamboats were moored, without bothering to take the haul downstream and out of the port. The average resident was just as careless. The river seemed a perfect place for disposing of trash and garbage. But the New Orleans custom was to tote the refuse over the levee and dump it onto the batture, without bothering to walk the few extra steps to throw it into the water where it would be swept away. The accumulation added to the city's olfactory woes.

Invasion, military occupation, hurricanes, floods, riots, conflagrations, New Orleans has experienced them all since Bienville founded the city in 1718. None brought the hopelessness and suffering that accompanied the great epidemics, especially those of 1832, 1853, 1858, and 1878. And no triumph was as important as the great deliverance in 1905.

After the arrival of the steamer *Constitution* on October 25, 1832, Parson Theodore Clapp found two men who had collapsed on the levee. Around them a crowd had gathered, but it melted away when Clapp took a closer look and opined that the pair was dying of Asiatic cholera. Thus came the first of the major outbreaks to occur after the city reached the 50,000 population mark. Before long the death toll was 500 a day. At one point gravediggers prepared a trench fifty-seven feet long, eight feet wide, and four feet deep. Into it went 300 bodies, adults being placed in rows, and available space filled in by the bodies of small children. In 1848 cholera claimed 1,646 lives, and in 1849 the toll rose to 3,176. While yellow fever doubtless existed earlier, it was only recognized in 1793, and the first epidemic was recorded in 1796, when there were 638 deaths in a population of only 8,756.

Authorities still had no clue to the cause of the spread of the fever when, in 1853, a city now grown to 150,000 was devastated by the worst of the outbreaks. Estimates of the number of refugees who headed over the lake ranged from 30,000 to 75,000. Twenty-seven thousand cases of yellow fever were recorded, with almost 8,000 deaths in the city.

By August 18 the terrifying death rate, nearly 300 a day, caused Mayor A. D. Crossman to order six-pounders set up in the principal squares and fifty rounds fired at sunrise and sunset. He halted the practice after two days because the booms sounded to the ill like death signals. There was no end, however, to the burning of barrels of tar at the major intersections.

Coffins piled up at cemeteries because gravediggers could not keep up with the incoming flow. Finally bodies were placed in graves scarcely a foot deep. When the Board of Health ordered immense quantities of tar to be set afire in the Lafayette Cemetery, the rumor spread that bodies were being burned. It was long before the age of Dixieland music and jazz funerals in New Orleans, but when musicians could be obtained, dirges were played as bodies were borne to burial places.

Yellow Jack returned in 1858, causing 4,856 deaths. In the summer of 1862 New Orleanians waited in vain for the fever to decimate the Federal occupation troops of General Benjamin F. Butler. But the Union blockade of the Mississippi prevented any

Nearly eight thousand people lost their lives during the 1853 yellow fever epidemic in New Orleans, the worst the city ever suffered. Night burials are shown here. Illustration from *History of the Yellow Fever*, an 1854 pamphlet, courtesy John Duffy.

vessel from entering the river, from May on. In the war years and immediately afterward, New Orleans was healthy, primarily because General Butler had effectively cleaned up the city, removing filth from streets and batture. New Orleans never had experienced such sanitation.

In 1878, a year after the end of Reconstruction, the fever struck again. This was the time when authorities believed that fumes from carbolic acid might be helpful, and a sea of the fluid was poured into gutters. The acid drained into the bayous and drainage canals with a resultant fish kill that complicated the general misery with putrid odors. As always, the affluent fled. But once the word of the epidemic was out, posses armed with shotguns and rifles gathered at railway stations in Hammond, Biloxi, Mobile, and other towns and prevented passengers from leaving trains out of New Orleans. The 1878 count was 27,000 ill and 4,406 deaths in a population now reaching 210,000.

At a meeting of the Orleans Parish Medical Society in 1901, Dr. Rudolph Matas called attention to the findings of Walter Reed and other American doctors in Havana, who proved Dr. Carlos Finlay's theory that yellow fever was spread by the bite of the *Aedes aegypti* mosquito. Matas proposed a study by the society, which determined that the mosquito was prevalent in New Orleans. As a result, authorities were prepared when cases of the fever were revealed in 1905. A campaign was begun to screen all of the residential cisterns from which citizens obtained their water. Oil was poured on puddles to prevent the hatching of mosquito eggs. And every time a case of fever was reported, a trained crew was sent to the home to put up screens over the doors and windows of the room where the patient was isolated. This reduced the possibility of the transmission of the fever to new victims. What started out as a major epidemic was halted abruptly, although 3,402 people fell sick and 452 deaths occurred before the preventive measures were in full operation. Never since has there been a serious yellow fever epidemic in the United States.

When bubonic plague cases surfaced in 1914, authorities knew that they originated through infected rats leaving incoming ships. The vector that spread the disease to humans was a flea or a bedbug that bit a rat and then people. At first an effort was made to isolate several thousand residents of an area near the center of the city where the disease was found. All businesses in the area were closed, and guards attempted to keep people from moving in or out. The plan was abandoned after a few hours. City officials then considered building a levee around the area and flooding it to drive out the rats. Finally, 622 ratcatchers baited 38,000 traps. In less than two months 30,000 rats were brought in and examined in a laboratory. One in a thousand was contaminated. The outbreak was ended with only ten deaths.

The first impression would be that the disease-ridden metropolis was an unlikely place to become an American medical center. Yet the vulnerability of a population that was multiplying in the early 1800s after the Louisiana Purchase provided an opportunity for footloose healers in the rest of the country who were having trouble finding patients. Down the river they came, trained physicians and surgeons, along with a large number of quacks and charlatans. The

Creole colony already had its own native practitioners, many of whom had been educated in Paris. They resented the influx of professional rivals whose qualifications they doubted. Conflicts inevitably developed. In addition to ill-feeling springing from the competition for patients, other differences split the two camps. The Creoles spoke French, the Americans English. And the American newcomers mostly practiced what was called heroic medicine. They attacked disease aggressively. They bled patients into unconsciousness, prescribed whopping doses of calomel or quinine. On the other hand, the Creoles used drugs sparingly and relied more on gentle nursing care to make a sick person well. Antagonisms persisted into the twentieth century. The division was so deep that not until 1878 could an enduring local medical association be formed by drawing members from both groups. It is the Orleans Parish Medical Society.

Despite strife and pestilence, the development of New Orleans as a medical mecca has continued until the present. The foundation was laid as early as 1736, when Charity Hospital was established at Chartres and Bienville streets with the help of a 10,000-livre legacy left by sailor and boatbuilder Jean Louis to provide a haven for sick seamen. One of the oldest hospitals in continuous operation in the country, Charity provided free care for the indigent long before the federal government came into the picture with its Medicaid and Medicare programs. Louisiana was a pioneer state in financing cradle to grave medical attention. The number of doctors who received their postgraduate training in Charity's busy wards runs into the many thousands.

No date is more important in this context than January 5, 1835. It was the birthday of the Medical College of Louisiana, begun by seven young New Orleans doctors, of whom only one was native-born. The college eventually became part of the University of Louisiana and then the Tulane University School of Medicine. Over a period of a century and a half no other institution has done so much to influence the practice of the healing arts in New Orleans.

In the atmosphere of tensions and antagonisms, it is not surprising that another medical school should have arisen in New Orleans as the result of a personal animosity. The board of administrators of the Tulane Educational Fund thwarted the hopes of Governor Huey P. Long for receiving an honorary degree from Tulane University. In retaliation, Long established in October, 1931, the Louisiana State University Medical School, which now trains most of the physicians who begin practice in the state. The Tulane medical school is on one side of the main Charity Hospital building facing on Tulane Avenue, the LSU school on the other.

When a newspaper, the *States-Item*, observed its centennial in 1977 by naming the New Orleanian Of The Century, it chose not a politician or an industrialist but a surgeon, Dr. Rudolph Matas, largely because of the importance of his influence in the conquest of yellow fever. Matas, recipient of the first Distinguished Service Award of the American Medical Association, was a towering figure in international medicine, an innovator whose work brought advances in vascular surgery, local anesthesia, and other areas of treatment. Upon Matas' retirement as professor of surgery at Tulane in 1927, he was succeeded by the only other New Orleans practitioner who ever was to attain a stature fully as great, and perhaps greater. Dr. Alton Ochsner was elected to the presidencies of more national and international medical societies than any other doctor who ever lived. He was the first eminent medical authority to warn against the health hazards of smoking cigarettes. He was the central figure in the founding and operation of the New Orleans medical complex that bears his name, Ochsner Medical Institutions. The Ochsner facility on Jefferson Highway is the magnet that draws one-half of the patients who travel to New Orleans for diagnosis and treatment. Thousands come from Latin America, where Ochsner's death brought headlines and eulogies, as it had in the United States.

J.W.

BIBLIOGRAPHY

Duffy, John, ed. *The Rudolph Matas History of Medicine in Louisiana*. 2 vols. Baton Rouge, 1958, 1962.

Wilds, John. *Crises, Clashes and Cures*. New Orleans, 1978.

16.

Life in New Orleans at the beginning of the twentieth century had settled into a pattern of relative simplicity and serenity, as compared with that in the raucous days of Reconstruction and the era following. Its people, with rich and varied ethnic backgrounds and a fondness for the fun and frolic of the good life, had grown into a populace whose appreciation of the old would always be in fashion.

In 1900, there were some two thousand saloons where a person could indulge in hard spirits, and but 148 precincts where he could cast a ballot. It was the day of free lunches in many barrooms; the electric streetcar was displacing the mule car; the horse and buggy was still the principal mode of transportation; and ceiling fans provided the only air conditioning. It was the time when jazz was born, and would soon join grand opera, theater, and vaudeville as a major cultural activity.

While the tensions of Reconstruction were about over, political factional wars were beginning to heat up. The economy had not regained its pre–Civil War heights when New Orleans was the second-wealthiest city in the nation, and it never would again. But the city was experiencing a steady growth—from 168,675 in 1860 to 287,104 in 1900. The port, which accounted for practically all the trade and business, was prospering.

Among many municipal problems, the city had one particularly nagging one. It had not conquered the threat of yellow fever epidemics, which at intervals in the previous century had wiped out large segments of the population. Not until 1905 did New Orleans health authorities begin to implement the recent discoveries concerning the fever's spread.

In 1905, when New Orleans had its last yellow fever outbreak, President Roosevelt visited the city in October, making the trip against the advice of his aides, who feared he might fall victim. The visit served the city well, since at that time neighboring states were ordering quarantines against New Orleans. Roosevelt's visit helped dispel fears and restore confidence in the city.

As the century dawned the port still was the principal factor in the city's economy and would remain so. But as the years moved on, oil and tourism have boosted its financial situation. Also, the city has played a leading role in sending men to outer space and to the moon, building the boosters for the huge, powerful Saturn rockets at its sprawling Michoud complex.

Because of its varied ethnic makeup, and a peculiar neighborhood racial housing pattern, New Orleans weathered the mid-century desegregation crises with less pain and disruption than that experienced in some other southern cities. Blacks and whites have lived in close proximity through the years, not segmented by a hypothetical dividing line. Thus, when integration was ordered the city fathers had a built-in head start.

In contrast to the easygoing day-by-day existence of its average citizens, however, New Orleans' twentieth-century political life has been marked by tumult and strife. Mayor Walter C. Flower was serving out his term as the new century began, and Paul Capdevielle held the chair for four years until 1904. Those early years saw the blossoming of machine politics, a development which was to have a profound effect upon the government of the community for nearly half a century.

The Regular Democratic Organization, which resembled Tammany Hall in New York, had slowly emerged as the city's most powerful political unit. Its strategy was directed by the Choctaw Club, which had seventeen leaders, one for each ward in the city. Once the bosses chose a candidate for public office, they directed the organization to give its precinct-by-precinct backing at the polls.

Coincident with the rise in power of the Choctaw Club was the emergence of a young politician from Algiers, Martin Behrman, who was elected mayor five times and became the dominant political figure in the first quarter-century. Behrman, leader of the Fifteenth Ward, had entered politics during the period when Republicans and Democrats were locked in a struggle for supremacy. As Republican influence waned during the bitter days of Reconstruction, the Democrats gained supremacy and the two-party system was practically destroyed. The city, and state, gradually developed a factional primary system within the Democratic party, a procedure that survived until the 1970s.

Behrman, elected in 1904, won the next three successive terms before being beaten by Andrew McShane in 1920. Behrman made a comeback in 1924 to win a fifth term, but died in office in December of 1926. He holds the record for length of service as mayor, a record made possible by the operation of the Regular machine. Success of the organization, which later became known as the Old Regulars, was credited to its simplicity of structure. Each ward leader would supervise his precinct captains, who saw to it that their supporters voted right.

The machine enforced its rule by the use of jobs from City Hall and lesser offices. Anyone hired was beholden to the machine and those who failed to support the machine lost their jobs. Patronage was the game. The system eventually infiltrated the public school system. Later, the citizenry forced the schools to be removed from partisan politics and placed under supervision of an independently elected board.

Behrman stabilized the city government and, although a product of the machine, brought about some reforms. In 1912 he led a movement to change the form of municipal government from a mayor and seventeen-member council (one from each ward) to a mayor and commission council of four at-large members. Shortly after his first election, the astute Behrman observed: "The electric car has knocked out the horse car and messenger boys have given way to the telephone, and just as surely politics is not what it used to be." Politics had indeed become a different game, and the pattern held until mid-century when another electronic marvel, television, contributed heavily to dismemberment of the political machine.

Behrman pushed development of the Industrial Canal, which connects the Mississippi River with Lake Pontchartrain and the Intracoastal Waterway, and later tied in with the Mississippi River—Gulf Outlet. The canal, which also provided locations for industry, was constructed under supervision of the man who built the Panama Canal, General George W. Goethals.

In 1924, in his famous "Papa's Coming Home" campaign, Behrman promised to build a seawall along the shores of Lake Pontchartrain to make possible reclamation of thousands of acres of land. He died before seeing this accomplished, but a succeeding administration carried out the plan.

Behrman and the Old Regular machine—the New Orleans Ring, as it became known—used both public works and political craftiness to help stay in office. The one-dollar poll tax, authorized by the 1921 state constitution to help disfranchise the Negro, became a handy election tool for the Old Regulars. Only qualified voters who had paid their poll taxes were permitted to vote. The Old Regulars saw to it that their followers and friends were eligible to vote, and voted, in those days of paper ballots.

Although he was the acknowledged master politician of his day, Behrman failed to detect unrest among the electorate in 1920, when he lost the mayoralty to McShane. His reluctance to close Storyville, where prostitution was permitted with official city sanction, was a factor. But Behrman could not be denied City Hall for long. His spirited campaign in 1924 put him back.

Behrman was succeeded by Arthur J. O'Keefe, a member of the council who served until July of 1929, when he resigned because of ill health. O'Keefe was succeeded by another councilman, T. Semmes Walmsley, who became acting mayor and then was elected to a four-year term.

Walmsley's tenure coincided with the rise to power of Huey P. Long as governor and United States senator from 1928 until September, 1935, when he was assassinated. Long had as much impact on New Orleans politics as any mayor who ever sat in the chair at

City Hall. A bitter enemy of the New Orleans Ring, as all referred to it, Long managed to do through manipulation of the legislature what he never was able to accomplish at the ballot box. Though he failed to carry the city in any election, he succeeded in conquering the municipal government.

The Old Regulars were his nemesis until he managed to break the machine's back and take over most of its members through defections. Long had won the governorship by putting together the votes of Protestant north and central Louisiana with those of Catholic southwest Louisiana. He united peoples of vast language, religious, and cultural differences into a voting majority, and did it mostly by campaigning against the vices of machine politics in New Orleans. The Old Regulars, never strong enough to elect their own candidates in statewide races, nevertheless could swing a victory for country faction candidates by use of their bloc vote. They had been doing this for many years until Long broke the pattern.

Without allies in the city government, Long went to the legislature, which he controlled, to pass laws that transferred the powers from city to state offices. Boasting that he could buy members of the legislature "like a sack of potatoes," Long had the lawmakers adopt statutes which authorized the state to take control of the police and fire departments, strip the city of its taxing powers, and take over election functions. Simultaneously, he create⌐ a bond and tax board empowered to handle municipal finances. It was a knockout blow to New Orleans and sent the city into virtual bankruptcy. Walmsley, reduced to a figurehead role, was called upon to resign, but he refused, vowing that he would not quit until the financial and political siege was lifted.

Long, as senator, had continued to run the state government through his handpicked successor, Governor O. K. Allen. After Long was assassinated, state government was thrown into chaos. His political heirs began to talk of making peace with the city. The turmoil continued for months, during which time Governor Allen died and was succeeded by Lieutenant Governor James A. Noe.

In the 1936 election, the Long machine spurned Noe, selecting instead an appellate judge from New Orleans, Richard W. Leche, as its candidate. Leche extended the olive branch to New Orleans. Walmsley, reelected in 1934 to a second four-year term, agreed to resign in midterm if the state would restore New Orleans' self-government. He left office in July, and Governor Leche called a special election to fill the vacancy. Before he did he saw to it that the Long forces agreed upon Walmsley's successor.

Robert S. Maestri, Louisiana conservation commissioner and businessman, and a principal Long supporter, was handpicked for the job. Maestri won the office without having to face the electorate. The Democratic party had set a primary date, and Maestri and a minor candidate qualified to run. The Long forces arranged for the minor candidate to withdraw; the Republicans did not offer a candidate for the general election. Whereupon the registrar of voters called off the primary and the general election, declaring Maestri elected. The Long forces then had the legislature extend the unexpired term for four years, giving Maestri a free ride for six years.

President Franklin D. Roosevelt visited the city shortly after Maestri took over. During Long's bitter political battles in the state and in Congress, Louisiana became estranged from the national government with the result that the flow of federal funds slowed to a trickle. With Long's death and the change in attitudes in Louisiana, the state and national administrations made peace. The FDR visit, which became popularly known as the Second Louisiana Purchase, brought about solid Louisiana support for the Roosevelt administration and touched off a flow of federal funds to the state for public works.

In the wake of the Long machine's demise, the Justice Department sent a special assistant attorney general, O. John Rogge, to New Orleans in answer to citizen demands, to take over an investigation into charges of widespread fraud against a number of Long machine lieutenants. Rogge directed the return of indictments and then prosecuted some of the leading politicians and businessmen in the city. In September of 1939, Rogge brought to trial Seymour Weiss, who had served as treasurer of the Long machine; Dr. James

President Franklin Delano Roosevelt waves good-bye to a crowd at the old L&N Railroad Station (at the foot of Canal Street) in 1937. *From left*: Governor Richard W. Leche, FDR, Mayor Robert S. Maestri, and Elliott Roosevelt, son of FDR. Photo by Wilfred L. d'Aquin.

Monroe Smith, president of Louisiana State University; and three others on mail fraud charges in connection with the sale to the state of the Bienville Hotel. This became known as the "double dip" trial because the principals, having sold the hotel including furnishings to the state, later resold to the state the furnishings after discovering they needed more money to divvy up among participants.

The tall, hard-driving Rogge showed a passion for prosecution as he stalked his defendants in the courtroom. For the first time in history, he used the mail fraud statutes in major criminal prosecution and won convictions. Rogge's actions caused a sensation in New Orleans and the state. After two trials in New Orleans, in which he also sent a group to prison in an Orleans Levee Board refinancing scheme, Rogge went after Governor Leche on a charge of fraud in the purchase of trucks for the state. He sent Leche to prison also.

The New Orleans political front, quiet during World War II, began to simmer as the war drew to a close and Maestri's term neared expiration. Maestri had put his business acumen to work, launching modest public improvement programs with federal aid and restoring the city's financial integrity. But his administration became embroiled in charges of payroll padding and inefficiency. Citizen groups, calling for an end to the old spoils system, urged adoption of civil service.

Maestri appeared well on his way to another term, however, when his leading opponent, former congressman J. O. Fernandez, withdrew from the race five days before the qualifying deadline. This enraged a group of citizens seeking a change at City Hall. They contacted a returning thirty-two-year-old army colonel, de-Lesseps S. Morrison, and offered to back him. Morrison accepted the challenge, put on a whirlwind campaign, and won. Morrison, who had cut his political teeth as a state representative prior to the war, then formed his own political organization and held onto the office through three other elections. He resigned with a year to go in his fourth term to become ambassador to the Organization of American States.

Morrison found corruption rife when he moved into City Hall. Gambling and prostitution flourished, hundreds of racehorse handbooks operated openly, as did thousands of slot machines. The police department faced widespread charges of payoffs. Morrison issued a strong antigambling order which sent the bookies to the back rooms and upper levels and made the prostitutes more cautious. Some slots were seized and dumped into the river, but the antigambling edict didn't stand for long. Morrison's new police superintendent resigned in disgust, and the police scandal charges remained. Gradually, the situation worsened. Not until Senator Estes Kefauver came to town with his crime investigating committee did the situation improve substantially. And, it remained for a conscientious state police superintendent, Francis Grevemberg, to bring a halt to most gambling and prostitution in a city that long had tolerated sin.

While mayor, Morrison yearned to be governor, running for the office three times in eight years and losing each time. It was a difficult time for a New Orleans mayor seeking statewide office, with desegregation clouding the political horizon. Morrison's tenure was marked by a number of reforms, including the establishment of civil service for city employees. He moved City Hall from the Greek-columned Gallier Hall on St. Charles Avenue to a new complex on Duncan Plaza bordering Loyola Avenue, built a new public library, paved many streets, and led the way in eliminating the city's 144 grade crossings in connection with building a new rail passenger terminal. The political climate created with the election of reform governor Sam H. Jones in 1940 had made it possible for Morrison to bring about changes in New Orleans' government.

Morrison frequently headed trade missions to Latin and South America, developing contacts which eventually led him into the ambassadorship. He was the dominant force in city government and became the strongest foe of Earl K. Long, brother of Huey, who inherited the Long mantle after Huey's death.

It was during Morrison's years that the National Aeronautics and Space Administration selected the Michoud industrial plant in eastern New Orleans as the site to assemble the rocket boosters which propelled the astronauts into orbit and to the moon. The Michoud project brought good times, since the federal complex employed more than ten thousand persons at high-level wages. The plant has operated at a reduced capacity in recent years.

One of the achievements in this era was the establishment of the University of New Orleans on lakefront land formerly occupied by the U.S. Naval Air Station. As a political campaign device, Governor Earl Long proposed establishment of the university and Morrison ultimately endorsed the idea. Dr. Homer L. Hitt, a professor and associate dean in the Louisiana State University system, of which UNO is a part, was chosen as the founding chancellor. In less than a quarter century, UNO grew into the state's second-largest university with an enrollment of more than 15,000 and won professional recognition.

During Morrison's second term, a citizens' committee succeeded in getting permission from the legislature to rewrite New Orleans' city charter. The new charter, still in effect, provides for a mayor, five district and two at-large council members. Morrison went along with a provision limiting a mayor to two successive terms. Later, he had second thoughts, and tried to have the limit removed in a referendum, but failed.

Upon Morrison's resignation, veteran councilman Victor H. Schiro was named interim mayor by the council, and then won two terms. He generally carried on Morrison's programs, adding some of his own, including the widening of Poydras Street, and headed off any major racial conflicts during desegregation. He served until 1970, when Moon Landrieu won the office. Landrieu, sensing the strength of an emerging black voting bloc, put together a coalition of black and white citizens that carried him to victory. He served two terms.

Under Landrieu the city pushed forward as dramatically as it had under Morrison. With Landrieu's help, the Louisiana Superdome, a state project, became a reality. The city's skyline, which had not shown much change since the days when the Hibernia tower was the principal landmark in the 1920s, began to grow.

As Landrieu ended his term, Ernest N. ("Dutch") Morial, an appellate court judge, took note of the fact that black voting strength was nearly equal to the white and turned aside several opponents to become the city's first black mayor. He started a trend, being succeeded by a black councilman, Sidney Barthelemy, and then by his eldest son, Marc, who served two terms and announced that he would to try to change the city charter to seek a third term. The elder Morial was the first African American to graduate from Louisiana State University Law School and the first elected to the legislature in the twentieth century.

One of the most significant developments in the twentieth century in New Orleans was the perfection of the city's drainage system by A. Baldwin Wood, superintendent of the Sewerage and Water Board. Wood developed a special pump which made it possible to move seas of water from the city quickly, pumping the water into Lake Pontchartrain and thus preventing flooding. The city, many parts of which are below sea level, would frequently flood—were it not for the series of canals and pumping stations which drain its saucerlike territory. (In recent years, heavy rains, which pour some sixty-five inches of water on the city annually, have caused flooding in some areas.) Wood has been recognized widely for his expertise. He assisted Holland in draining the Zuyder Zee and installed a pumping system in the Dutch East Indies.

New Orleans' size has declined since 1960, when the head count was 627,525. By 1970, the census showed a decline to 593,471, and by 2000 to 484,674 as whites fled the city principally to avoid desegregation in the public school system. Since 1950, most of the metropolitan area expansion has taken place in adjoining Jefferson and St. Bernard parishes. But the eastern New Orleans section has been drained and developed in recent years, converting a vast swampland into a modern community of new boulevards, homes, and businesses. Meanwhile, the population of adjoining parishes has increased rapidly, to the point where the metropolitan area count stands a approximately 1.3 million.

The city, a favored convention and tourist spot, has witnessed a boom in construction of hotels and other facilities to entertain visitors. Its municipal problems brought on by a weak tax base and lack of heavy industry continue to be the subjects of almost daily controversy, but the natives have learned to take it in stride and visitors become amused at the unfolding political drama.

The tenor of life is greatly akin to that of the more placid days when the century was born. People move to New Orleans from Texas, Mississippi, Alabama, and other southern states, from the North, the Northeast, Midwest, and Far West. On arrival, they generally complain about how so many things are different, but after a few months are absorbed into New Orleans' traditions and became involved in its varied activities. A different kind of fever grips them as they turn out for Mardi Gras parades, jazz funerals, and festivals. They begin considering themselves natives.

There are now nearly three thousand barrooms and other locations dispensing liquor, and 428 precincts where voters ballot by machine instead of paper tickets. The demographics may have changed, but the tradition remains true to history. New Orleans long ago decided it would be a different American city, and apparently intends to stay that way.

W.G.C.

BIBLIOGRAPHY

Behrman, Martin. An address, Members' Council, Association of Commerce, New Orleans, May 15, 1919.

Kemp, John R. *Martin Behrman of New Orleans: Memoirs of a City Boss.* Baton Rouge, 1977.

Haas, Edward F. *DeLesseps S. Morrison and the Image of Reform.* Baton Rouge, 1974.

Item, April 24, 1925; March 11, 1936; August 8, 1938.

States, September 17, 1936.

States-Item, May 7, 1974; January 20, 1978.

Times-Picayune, April 28, 1907. Sunday Magazine, May 12, 1918.

Williams, Robert Webb. "Martin Behrman: Mayor and Political Boss of New Orleans, 1904–26." M.A. thesis, Tulane University, 1952.

17.

 ANDREW JACKSON HIGGINS

The ingenuity of a New Orleans boatbuilder who made it possible to put America's fighting forces on enemy beaches during World War II won Andrew Jackson Higgins a place in history.

Pushed out of the European mainland by quick-striking German forces, the Allied high command was faced with the necessity to retake the Continent and liberate France and other occupied countries. A similar situation existed in the Pacific Ocean, where Japan had captured many islands.

Invasion was the only way. The Allies decided to strike from bases in England across the English Channel, and from the open sea in the Pacific, delivering troops in huge transports supported by air power. But how could they get their forces from ship to shore, closing a gap created by the large vessels' inability to maneuver in shallow water? That gap was a monumental problem.

Andrew Jackson Higgins, named for the famous general who had successfully defended New Orleans in 1815, provided the answer. How did it happen? Higgins, in the lumber business and a longtime builder of small boats, in 1937 pioneered the design of a craft that could operate in shallow water, run over obstacles and upon beaches to pick up logs, then back off rapidly. At the time, Higgins was working a stand of timber in swampy areas. His boat, a snub-nosed craft, was equipped with a hinged front that would fold down to provide a ramp for unloading. He called the vessel the Eureka.

When the United States Army was made aware of the Higgins boat, it became interested, as did Higgins in the problems faced by the army and navy. Eventually, Higgins built several models of landing craft to fit specific needs, but the Eureka was a workhorse and served as the primary model for these craft. To assure maneuverability, Higgins recessed the bottom in a center funnel-like tunnel that shielded the drive shaft.

The army and navy ordered thousands of the boats, each of which could carry some three dozen fully equipped men from ship to shore. Higgins expanded his factory from a small one on St. Charles Avenue to a large operation in City Park and later to the Industrial Canal. He built 20,094 landing craft during the war, plus 215 PT (patrol) boats.

President Franklin D. Roosevelt was so impressed by Higgins that he personally visited him on September 29, 1942, having his railcar switched into the City Park plant, where he toured the facility and addressed the hard-hatted workers. And after the war President Dwight D. Eisenhower told his biographer, Stephen Ambrose, that Higgins had "won the war" by making it possible to put troops ashore quickly during the invasions at Normandy and other beaches. General Douglas MacArthur offered a similar compliment.

Bombastic and well known for being outspoken in his dealings with Washington bureaucracy as well for his untiring zeal to get a job done, Higgins was born in Columbus, Nebraska, on August 28, 1886. His family moved to Omaha when he was a child.

When interviewed by this writer while a reporter for the New Orleans *Item* in the late 1930s, Higgins recalled that he had built his first boat at the age of twelve in the basement of his family's Omaha home. He chuckled as he recalled that the boat, built for sailing on ice, was too large to move through a door or window, so he had to knock out a wall to get it out.

That was the beginning of a career that took him, with his interest in lumber exporting and boats, from Omaha to Mobile, Alabama, and in 1910 to New Orleans, where he went from obscurity to fame. During the war, U.S. maritime commissioner

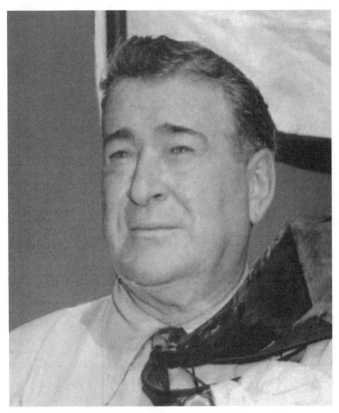

Andrew Jackson Higgins, the New Orleans boatbuilder who gained fame in World War II. Courtesy of the *Times-Picayune.*

John Carmody observed that Higgins was "taking [his] place beside the great production geniuses of the modern time," and Great Britain's Lord Mountbatten said that "without the boats Higgins is manufacturing the combined operations command could not exist."

A coauthor of this book got a personal glimpse of the enormity of Higgins' efforts. O. K. LeBlanc, a Marines rifle company commander at Guadalcanal, Tarawa, and Saipan, says that he was con-

Backing up on the beaches, a Higgins landing craft could lower its rear panel, load men and equipment, and take off within minutes. Capacity was three dozen men. Press Association, Inc., photo published in the Eureka News Bulletin, Higgins Industries, November 1943. Now contained in the David R. McGuire Papers, Special Collections, Tulane University Library.

stantly aware of Higgins and New Orleans. "I found myself scrambling down the side of the APA Crescent City (a transport), gripping a cargo net and then dropping down into a bobbing Higgins boat time after time en route to bloody beaches," said LeBlanc. "Much has been written about the invasions, but not enough about Higgins' boats, which put us in positions to fight."

W.G.C.

BIBLIOGRAPHY

Cowan, Walter G. Interviews with Higgins while a reporter for the New Orleans *Item.*

Magee, L. Phillip. "Helping Higgins Help Us All." *The Orange Disk*, Sept.–Oct. 1943, Vol. 6, No. 5.

Strahan, Jerry E. *Andrew Jackson Higgins and the Boats that Won World War II.* Baton Rouge, 1994.

Part III

The Flavor of the City

Part II

18.

❧ MARDI GRAS ❧

What is Mardi Gras?

It's French for Fat Tuesday.

But what's Fat Tuesday?

It is the day before Ash Wednesday, the first day of the penitential season of Lent. Mardi Gras is the last day of the pre-Lenten Carnival season in New Orleans.

Although Mobile has Carnival, and a good one, too—indeed, Carnival as it is celebrated today in New Orleans was imported from Mobile—neither it nor any other festival in the United States can compare with the New Orleans Carnival that reaches a tremendous climax on Mardi Gras.

It is an old New Orleans saying that half the town will turn out to see the other half parade. During the Carnival parade season half the people really don't parade, but just about half the city does indeed turn out to see those who are parading.

In and around New Orleans, about fifty Carnival organizations stage parades with floats and maskers during the twelve-day period that winds up on Mardi Gras. On that day, a half million people jam Canal Street for the parades of Rex, King of Carnival, Zulu, and two truck parades. And tens of thousands of men, women, children, and even babes in arms, line Rex's six-mile parade route leading to Canal Street.

Mardi Gras is a day that must be seen to be believed, must be experienced in order to understand it. It is a day of fun and frolic, good-humored camaraderie—a day on which a community in the nation lets go. Indeed, a psychiatrist might well consider Mardi Gras a safety valve, important for the city's mental health. Carnival is also what New Orleanians call the greatest free show on earth, for it is staged by the dues-paying members of the many organizations, each of which exists for itself and for its Carnival presentation, whether it be a parade or a ball, or both.

And an aspect of Carnival not usually recognized, or fully appreciated, is that it represents at least a $15 million part of the city's economy—New Orleans money spent in New Orleans. There is also, of course, an important impact on tourism in New Orleans, but it must be stressed that Carnival never was conceived as "tourist bait," and never has existed as such. If not a single tourist came to New Orleans during Carnival it would have no effect on the twelve-day parade extravaganza which culminates spectacularly on Mardi Gras.

What is the date of Mardi Gras? That is a question often asked by visitors. The answer is that Mardi Gras is a movable date which may fall as early as February 3 and as late as March 9. It was as long ago as 1818 that Mardi Gras was on February 3, and it will not occur again until the twenty-second century. Mardi Gras last fell on March 9 in 1943. It will not come on that date again until 2038.

Why is Mardi Gras a movable date? Because it is the day before Ash Wednesday, which is forty-six days—forty days plus six Sundays—before Easter. And Ash Wednesday is movable because Easter is a movable feast. And here is how it is all determined: Easter is the first Sunday after the full moon that follows the spring equinox, March 21. Forty-six days back is thus Ash Wednesday and the forty-seventh day back is Mardi Gras.

It is interesting to note that the first place-name on the map of Louisiana was Mardi Gras. In 1699, Iberville entered the Mississippi River on Mardi Gras, March 3, and he camped on the banks of a little bayou, seventy-five miles downriver from the site of New Orleans. He named the stream Bayou Mardi Gras, and the little point of land formed by its entry into the river he called Mardi Gras Point.

Tens of thousands of people line New Orleans streets for the Mardi Gras parades.
Photo by A. J. Meek.

While during the French and Spanish regimes in Louisiana, New Orleans was the scene of balls and fetes during the pre-Lenten season, there is no documentary evidence of a parade on Mardi Gras until 1837. For twenty years these annual parades were of a do-it-yourself nature, that is, there wasn't any planned theme and one was free to follow along in a carriage, on a horse, or on foot.

Informality was the rule and with it there crept into the procession rowdyism of the worst sort. Throwing things to the parade throngs is a Carnival tradition in New Orleans. The maskers toss from the moving floats beads, aluminum medallions, called doubloons, and other trinkets. At every parade this custom evokes a multithousand-voice chorus: "Hey, Mister, throw me something!"

But it was throwing that set off the clamor for the abolition of the Mardi Gras celebration in New Orleans in the 1850s. The original parade of 1837 featured the tossing of candies, fruit, and other sweetmeats—to the delight of the crowd. Subsequently, practical jokers in the parade began to bring little bags of flour, with which they pelted their friends along the route. It wasn't long before flour-tossing became general at a Mardi Gras parade, with the spectators throwing back at the maskers. When pieces of brick were inserted in the bags, rowdyism was in full swing and violence was not far behind. Thinking members of the public joined the press and city fathers to condemn the abuses and a considerable number called for the abolition of the festival, which they asserted was conceived in a barbarous age and had no place in the enlightened society of the 1850s.

Then it was, in 1857, that an organized Carnival group appeared, calling itself the Mistick Krewe of Comus, and it saved Mardi Gras from dying in disgrace. Six Mobilians who had settled in New Orleans were the driving force behind the Comus organization. They invented the word *krewe*, by giving a pseudo–Old English twist to *crew*, chose the god of revelry as their "patron saint," and, for good measure, spelled *mystic* as an Elizabethan poet might have spelled it.

The emergence of Comus on Mardi Gras night in 1857 created the form and pattern of Carnival parades as they still exist. Mardi Gras thus not only escaped oblivion but took a new lease on life,

"Hey, Mister, throw me something!" At Carnival parades maskers on the floats have beads and doubloons (throws) which they toss to the throngs along the route. Photo by A. J. Meek.

with the Comus parade and ball that followed.

In 1870 the Mistick Krewe was joined by the Twelfth Night Revelers in both a parade and a ball. This organization, which officially opens the Carnival season on January 6, the Feast of the Epiphany, ceased parading after several years, but still is in existence and its ball is one of Carnival's most prestigious.

The Rex organization, which calls its ruler King of Carnival, had an impromptu debut in 1872. When it became known that the Russian Grand Duke Alexis would be in New Orleans for Mardi Gras, a group of young businessmen hurriedly organized a day parade in honor of the Romanov prince. To be Rex, King for a Day, is the highest civic honor that can be bestowed upon a New Orleanian.

That same year, but on New Year's Eve, so it was really part of the 1873 Carnival season, the Knights of Momus rode forth for the first time under their banner and device, *Dum Vivimus, Vivamus* (While we're living, let's live it up). After a few years of parading on New Year's Eve, the Knights of Momus—their patron is the god of ridicule and raillery—settled on the Thursday night before Mardi Gras, but eventually quit parading.

The last of the surviving nineteenth-century parading organizations—there were a number that began and died—is the Krewe of Proteus, which started in 1882. In borrowing Comus' word *krewe,* Proteus started the trend that made krewe the generic term for all Carnival organizations. Proteus, the Old Man of the Sea, was a quick-change artist whose name became the English word *protean,* changeable. The organization parades on the Monday night before Fat Tuesday.

The next of the still existing parading krewes to emerge was Zulu, a black organization, which first paraded in 1909. Zulu, in the twenty-first century, is still going strong.

There are three periods to Carnival's growth: (1) From 1857, when Comus made its debut, to World War I; (2) Between the two world wars, when there was a proliferation of krewes, many of which staged both parades and balls, and when ladies' organizations were introduced; (3) From World War II to the present, when there was a second "population explosion" among Carnival krewes, many of them in the parishes (counties) adjacent to New Orleans.

Questions often asked are: How is Carnival coordinated? and How is Carnival subsidized? The answers are the same: it isn't. Each Carnival organization exists independently of all the others, and whether it is big or little, new or old, what a krewe does is, for its members, the BIG moment of the year. The city grants parade permits and recognizes traditional parade dates, and police patrol the parade route. Other than that, there isn't any coordination at all. Each krewe merely carries on, year after year, as it has done in the past. As for subsidies, the financing of a krewe's activity comes solely from its members, who pay dues, which in the aggregate pay all the krewe's bills.

Each year, at Municipal Auditorium alone there are more than sixty Carnival balls; the cost of production for each may run anywhere from $25,000 to $100,000, and in a few instances considerably higher. The balls represent at least $3 million of the $15 million segment of the New Orleans economy mentioned earlier. The fifty parades, in and about New Orleans, could easily equal that amount in production costs. Krewe favors and silver doubloons, which maskers give to the ladies they call out to the floor to dance during a ball, can reach a fantastic figure when it is considered that the average ball has about 250 members, who'll buy anywhere from six to ten favors at a cost of between $15 and $25 each. The throws—the word *throw* in Carnivalese means the beads, doubloons, plastic trinkets, chewing gum, and candy that maskers toss to the crowd—represent another significant piece of the economy. About ten thousand maskers, an average of two hundred for fifty parades, will add at least $2 million to the total.

But these production costs of Carnival—remember, all borne by the various krewe members—are only half the story. The amount of money put into circulation in New Orleans as a by-product of Carnival is also a fantastic figure. It is spent on evening clothes for men and women; in beauty parlors; for food and drink at krewe parties; for the beer, soft drinks, cotton candy, peanuts, hot dogs, hamburgers sold by street vendors; for costumes and masks for adult street maskers as well as children on Mardi Gras; for laundry and dry cleaning of starched shirts and evening wear for men and women; and for other things incidental to the ball season in general and the parade season in particular.

Smarting under an anti-discrimination law adopted in 1993, three of the oldest krewes—Proteus, Momus, and Comus—canceled their parades. Quickly, their dates for parading were grabbed by other organizations, but after a seven-year absence, Proteus returned to its Monday night slot. Thus a full schedule of parades remains, and parades have spread to nearby Jefferson Parish, which frolics as wildly as Orleans Parish during the festive week before Ash Wednesday. Actually, the neighborhood parades begin some three weeks before the finale on Shrove Tuesday.

Every Mardi Gras brings tens of thousands of people who want to experience what it is like to mingle with the crowds watching the parades each year. For those planning a visit to New Orleans at Mardi Gras in the near future, here are some dates:

2001	February 27	2011	March 8
2002	February 12	2012	February 21
2003	March 4	2013	February 12
2004	February 24	2014	March 4
2005	February 8	2015	February 17
2006	February 28	2016	February 9
2007	February 20	2017	February 26
2008	February 5	2018	February 13
2009	February 24	2019	March 5
2010	February 16	2020	February 25

C.L.D and W.G.C.

BIBLIOGRAPHY

A Chronicle of the First Century of the Knights of Momus. New Orleans, 1971.

Dufour, Charles L. *Krewe of Proteus: The First Hundred Years.* New Orleans, 1981.

Dufour, Charles L., and Leonard V. Huber. *If Ever I Cease to Love.* New Orleans, 1970.

La Cour, Arthur B. *New Orleans Masquerade.* Gretna, 1952.

Young, Perry. *The Mistick Krewe.* Originally published 1931. New Orleans, 1959.

19.

RELIGION

The steeples everywhere thrust heavenward. The skyline itself bears witness to the influence of the Church in the lives of New Orleanians.

More than half of the white children attend Roman Catholic schools. Hundreds of thousands of adults learned their ABCs from nuns, who for years rode free on streetcars and buses in perpetual recognition of their merciful ministrations in times of pestilence.

Louisiana's civil law, based on the Napoleonic Code, reflects Catholic teachings about such matters as the sanctity of the family. Forced heirship and community property provisions are intended to weld father, mother, and offspring into an indivisible unit.

Friday remains fish day in countless homes, long after the Church ceased to ban the eating of meat then. Lent brings a falling off in the number of customers at restaurants and places of amusement, although abstinence no longer is observed to the extent it once was. Nowadays, in contrast to the past, business does not virtually cease on Good Friday.

The community developed an easygoing tolerance in matters of private conduct, and generations of Catholics grew up not considering gambling and drinking as stops on the road to perdition. As a consequence, in New Orleans it's live and let live, an attitude which makes it unique among American cities.

It was inevitable that New Orleans would become one of the

most Catholic of American cities. The settlers were French, the rulers early on were Spanish, and the waves of later immigrants—Acadians, Germans, Irish, and Italians—all came from Catholic countries. Protestant worship developed with the arrival of the Kaintocks after the Louisiana Purchase and, in modern times, with the flow of restless Americans from Mississippi and other states.

In New Orleans, Catholics and Protestants lived amicably a century and more before the ecumenical movement was launched. In an atmosphere of religious good will, anti-Semitism never became a factor in the life of the city. For more than a century Jewish philanthropists have contributed notably to the communal well-being.

New Orleanians of all faiths joined together in 1987 to welcome Pope John Paul II, who made an historic visit to the city as part of an American tour. His one-day, two-night stay was highlighted by an open-air Mass that attracted many thousands to the lakefront campus of the University of New Orleans.

Although the French engineer Adrien de Pauger had, in laying out New Orleans, reserved for a church a site facing the Place d'Armes, it was not until 1727 that the first religious structure was completed. It was dedicated to Louis IX, the sainted king of France. Pauger designed the church, but died before it was finished and opened for services.

In that same year, there occurred an event of great religious significance for the Church in New Orleans. Ursuline nuns arrived on August 6, 1727, to establish a school for girls and to tend the hospital. After more than 250 years of unbroken service, the Ursulines are the oldest institution in New Orleans and, indeed, in the Mississippi Valley. Among the six Ursuline nuns was an eighteen-year-old novice, Sister Marie Madeleine of St. Stanislas. Sister Marie Madeleine, who before her profession was Madeleine Hachard of Rouen, wrote a series of letters to her father in which, with youthful exuberance, she described New Orleans. "I can assure you that I do not seem to be on the Mississippi, there is so much of magnificence and politeness as in France. . . . Cloth of gold and velours are commonplace here, albeit three times dearer than at Rouen. . . . The women here, as elsewhere, employ powder and rouge to conceal the wrinkles in their faces; indeed, the demon here possesses a great empire."

Religion, throughout the eighteenth century, played a significant role in New Orleans life. The relaxed attitude of both the clergy and the Catholic Creoles regarding observance of the Sabbath exercised an important influence in the spirit of tolerance for which New Orleanians became noted. Their obligation to attend mass on Sunday fulfilled, the Creoles felt free to indulge in a variety of harmless pleasures, which in the early nineteenth century shocked newly arrived Americans. As one American clergyman observed, although "priests are never seen . . . at balls, theaters, private dancing parties, or operas even . . . they do not teach that these amusements, abstractly considered, are sinful." Nor did they inveigh against gambling or drinking per se, even when they condemned excess.

New Orleans, under the French and Spanish, was far from straitlaced and one can understand why Anglo-Saxon Protestant newcomers were scandalized by what they considered the profanation of the Sabbath by the Creoles. To these austere Yankees, New Orleans was a city of godlessness and depravity. It is interesting to note, in contrast, two early legislative acts in New Orleans respecting Sunday observance. The Code Noir (Black Code), promulgated in 1724, established Roman Catholicism as the official religion of Louisiana and imposed on masters the obligation to provide religious instruction for their slaves and to observe strictly Sunday and holy days. A year earlier, in 1723, a New Orleans ordinance read: "It is also forbidden to play billiards on Sunday and . . . feast days . . . under penalty of a fine of one hundred livres, both against the keeper of the billiard room and against the players."

There had been, however, a climate of religious dissension during the last years of the French regime. The conflict over administrative jurisdiction between the Jesuits and the Capuchins continued for a number of years and only ended in 1763, when the French government ordered the suppression of the Jesuits in Louisiana. They were not reestablished until the third decade of the

The third church to be built on this site, St. Louis Cathedral is one of the most famous churches in the United States. It was completed in 1851. The first church was built in 1727. Photo by A. J. Meek.

nineteenth century. Later, the Catholic populace was divided into
two camps by the presence in New Orleans of the Spanish priest,
Father Antonio de Sedella, whom some saw as a tool of the Inquisition and others as a dedicated churchman, devoted to the spiritual
care of his congregation. As the popularity of this controversial
priest grew among the Creoles he became known, not as Padre
Antonio, but as Père Antoine. He died greatly beloved.

There were only two churches in New Orleans in 1803, when it
became an American city. One of these was the Cathedral Church of
St. Louis and the other was the chapel of the Ursulines. That there
was great laxity among the Creoles in the practice of their religion
cannot be denied. When Louisiana's first bishop, Luis Peñalver y
Cardenas, arrived in New Orleans in July of 1795 he was shocked
at the low state of religion and morals. Bishop Peñalver reported:
"The inhabitants do not listen to, or if they do, they disregard all
exhortations to maintain in its orthodoxy the Catholic faith and to
preserve the innocence of life. . . . No more than about the fourth
part of the population of the town ever attends Mass. . . . Fasting
on Fridays, and in Lent . . . is a thing unknown."

For almost three and a half decades, the original Church of St.
Louis served as the parish church of New Orleans, but by 1763 it
had fallen into such disrepair that it had to undergo extensive
renovations. When the great fire of 1788 swept the city, the church
went up in flames. Five years went by before the new church, the
gift of the wealthy Spanish official, Don Andrés Almonester y
Roxas, was completed. Spared in New Orleans' second devastating
fire in 1794, the church was dedicated as a cathedral and used for
the first time on Christmas Eve, 1794. It was this church that
served New Orleans at the time of the Louisiana Purchase. Having
again fallen into great disrepair, the cathedral was replaced in 1851
by the present structure.

Religion among the city's Protestants was, after the Louisiana
Purchase, a private and personal affair. There was no Protestant
church, no Protestant congregation, no Protestant minister in
New Orleans. Following an appeal in the *Louisiana Gazette* that the
city's Protestants demonstrate that they were not irreligious, a

meeting was held on May 30, 1805, to establish a Protestant church. Subscription lists were opened to support Christ Church, as it was named; a vote determined that the minister to be invited would be an Episcopalian The first organized Protestant service in New Orleans was held on Sunday, July 15, 1805, in a private home on Royal Street.

An appeal to Bishop Benjamin Moore of New York resulted in the dispatch to New Orleans of twenty-nine-year-old Philander Chase, who was installed as rector of Christ Church, which would not have a permanent home until 1816, when a church was built on Canal Street at Bourbon Street. Some years later, a second Christ Church was built there, and still later a third was erected on the corner of Canal and Dauphine. The present Christ Church Cathedral, on St. Charles Avenue, dates from 1886.

Throughout the nineteenth century, Episcopal churches sprang up in various parts of the city and in suburban towns, which one by one were absorbed into New Orleans. One of these was Trinity Church, still standing on Jackson Avenue, from the pulpit of which Bishop Leonidas Polk went forth to become a Confederate lieutenant general during the Civil War. Bishop Polk, a West Point graduate, was asked by a parishioner: "What! You, a bishop, throw off the gown for the sword?" Polk replied: "I buckle on the sword over the gown." Polk was killed at Pine Mountain, Georgia, on June 14, 1864. He was buried in Augusta, but in 1945 his remains were brought to New Orleans and interred under the choir floor in Christ Church Cathedral.

The second Protestant denomination installed in New Orleans was the Presbyterian church, which stemmed from preliminary efforts by the missionary Elias Cornelius in 1818. A Presbyterian church was built on St. Charles Street, between Gravier and Union streets, and was dedicated on July 4, 1820. Its second pastor was the Reverend Theodore Clapp, whose ministry in New Orleans lasted thirty-five years. When his questioned orthodoxy resulted in charges of heresy in 1833, Dr. Clapp was excommunicated by the Mississippi Presbytery. He became a Unitarian, and a large part of his congregation remained with him. Dr. Clapp's church was par-

St. Louis Cathedral, interior. Photo by A. J. Meek.

ticularly appealing to visitors and it came to be known as the Strangers' Church. It was a popular saying in New Orleans in the mid-nineteenth century that the first things that visitors in the city attended were "the American theater, the French Opera and Parson Clapp's Church."

After the division of Dr. Clapp's church, the Presbyterians held services in a warehouse facing Lafayette Square, on which site an imposing church was built in 1835. For more than forty years, the Reverend Benjamin M. Palmer presided over the pulpit. He was described by a contemporary as "a man of magnificent intellect, of superb forcefulness of logic, of golden rhetoric . . . of comprehensive, massive sympathies and a broad view of life." It was his two-hour sermon late in 1860 which greatly influenced New Orleans' sentiment for secession.

There were Baptists in New Orleans as early as 1812, when a group met for services in a private home. As early as 1826, attempts to establish a Baptist church were under way, but it wasn't until 1843 that the First Baptist Church was organized. The first church was situated on St. Charles Street, but financial difficulties resulted in a sheriff's sale in 1851. A new church was built at Camp and Terpsichore streets in 1854. Today, the First Baptist Church of New Orleans, situated on St. Charles Avenue and General Pershing Street, is one of the largest congregations in the South.

Almost half the churches in and about New Orleans in the closing decades of the twentieth century are Baptist churches. There are many black congregations, stemming from missionary activities among the freed slaves following the Civil War.

Methodism came to New Orleans as early as 1812, but the Carondelet Methodist Episcopal Church was not organized until 1825. The church, built at Carondelet and Poydras in 1836, burned in 1849. Other Methodist churches have been built in various sections of the city during the last half of the twentieth century.

While Protestantism, especially among the new arrivals in New Orleans, continued to spread, Irish immigrants in the 1830s and others from continental Europe swelled the Catholic population and new churches were needed. Thus were born "national" churches—St. Patrick's for the Irish, St. Alphonsus for the Germans, and St. Mary's for the Italians.

Although the 1724 Code Noir excluded Jews from Louisiana, there is no evidence that there were any Jews in New Orleans at the time of the promulgation of the code. Father Charles E. O'Neill, in his authoritative *Church and State in French Colonial Louisiana*, states that "if there were Jews present in Louisiana, there is no evidence that the expulsion paragraph of the code was ever invoked or executed." This same historian concludes that "possibly there were a few Jewish settlers in Louisiana from 1720 on."

While the Spanish tolerated Jews in Louisiana, it was not until after the Louisiana Purchase that they came to New Orleans in substantial numbers. In the nineteenth century waves of German immigrants, including many Jewish professional men and their families, came to New Orleans. Among the handful of pre–American regime Jews in New Orleans was Judah Touro, who purchased in 1847 the second Christ Church, situated on Canal and Bourbon streets, to serve as the city's first synagogue. From this pioneer Jewish congregation, synagogues spread to various sections of the city so that today New Orleans has no fewer than eight Jewish congregations. Touro, who came to New Orleans as a young man, was seriously wounded in the Battle of New Orleans. But he survived to become one of the city's wealthiest merchants and philanthropists. With matchless ecumenical spirit, he paid off the overdue $50,000 mortgage on Dr. Clapp's Unitarian church, asking nothing in return.

There are more than 850 places of worship in New Orleans, used by more than seventy different Christian denominations and by Islamic, Buddhist, Bahis, and Unification groups. Naturally, New Orleans' 850 churches are of various ages, but at least 15 of them are more than a hundred years old, and some of these are among the finest brick churches in America. A distinguished architectural historian, Nathaniel C. Curtis, wrote that "1850 to 1860 was a period when brick masons of rare skill flourished in New Orleans." Continuing in his *New Orleans: Its Old Houses, Shops and Public Buildings*, Curtis states: "This is evident when we examine the churches . . . which are built entirely of brick and in which architectural forms and details appropriate to brick have been devised and employed with an intelligence superior to that shown in any later work. In fact, it may be said with probable truth that as examples of the organic expression of brick architecture these edifices are hardly equalled by any elsewhere in the United States, and are fairly comparable to the latter Fifteenth Century brick churches of Rome."

Here is a list of New Orleans' century-old churches:

1826–1827   Our Lady of Guadaloupe, 411 North Rampart Street. (Originally a mortuary chapel for burial of yellow fever victims; Catholic.)

1840   St. Patrick's, 724 Camp Street. (Catholic.)

1841–1842   St. Augustine's, St. Claude Avenue at Governor Nicholls Street. (Catholic.)

1849   St. Theresa's, Camp and Erato streets. (Catholic.)

1848–1860   Sts. Peter and Paul, 2317 Burgundy Street. (Catholic.)

1852–1853   Trinity Church, Jackson Avenue at Coliseum Street. (Episcopal.)

1853   Holy Trinity Church, 721 St. Ferdinand Street. (Catholic.)

1855–1857   St. Alphonsus, 2029 Constance Street. (Catholic.)

1858–1859   Holy Redeemer Church, 2122 Royal Street. (Originally the Third Presbyterian Church; now Catholic.)

1858–1860   St. Mary's Assumption, Josephine and Constance streets. (Catholic.)

1866   St. Vincent de Paul, 3051 Dauphine Street. (Catholic.)

1869–1872   St. John the Baptist, 1139 Dryades Street. (Catholic.)

1875   St. Roch's Chapel, St. Roch Avenue between Derbigny and Roman streets. (Catholic.)

1875   Rayne Memorial Methodist Church, 3900 St. Charles Avenue.

1877   St. Stephen's, Napoleon Avenue and Camp Street. (Catholic.)

C.L.D.

BIBLIOGRAPHY

Baudier, Roger. *The Catholic Church in Louisiana*. New Orleans, 1939.

Carter, Hodding, and Betty Werlein Carter. *So Great a Good: A History of the Episcopal Church in Louisiana and of Christ Church Cathedral*. Sewanee, Tenn., 1955.

Curtis, Nathaniel C. *New Orleans: Its Old Houses, Shops and Public Buildings*. Philadelphia, 1933.

Leveque, J. M. "The Churches." In *Standard History of New Orleans*, ed. Henry Rightor. New York, 1900.

O'Neill, Charles E. *Church and State in French Colonial Louisiana*. New Haven, 1966.

20.

 MUSIC

New Orleans, a city chock-full of contradictions and surprises, was the first permanent home of grand opera in America and the birthplace of jazz. Throughout the nineteenth century, New Orleans established itself as a musical center for opera and concerts, but with the turn of the twentieth century, jazz began its evolution from the folk melodies and rhythms of the slaves into a new and original art form, which eventually became international.

The musical history of New Orleans begins in 1796, when the first recorded performance of an opera, Grétry's *Silvain*, was held. That there were earlier performances of opera cannot be doubted, but there is no documentation to prove it. Opera grew in popularity with the growth of New Orleans and a golden age flourished in the 1840s, when the Orleans Theater presented an incredible list of American premieres of operas by Meyerbeer, Halévy, Bellini, and Donizetti.

Concerts by international artists were a frequent feature of the "season" in New Orleans. Notable appearances were those of Jenny Lind, the Swedish Nightingale; the famed violinists, Ole Bull of Norway and Henri Vieuxtemps of Belgium; and the eighteen-year-old diva, Adelina Patti. In the 1840s, Bull and Vieuxtemps, amazingly, were in New Orleans at the same time and in a two-week period they gave a total of eleven concerts to full houses. Vieuxtemps performed at the Orleans Theater in the Vieux Carré and Bull at the St. Charles Theater, located above Canal Street. Thus New Orleans, a city of less than 120,000, supported with enthusiasm the two most famous violinists of their day.

Brought to New Orleans in 1851 by P. T. Barnum—the same who became a famous circus impresario—Jenny Lind, the Swedish Nightingale, gave fourteen concerts in the space of three weeks and all before packed houses. A third musical event of significance came on the eve of secession, when the eighteen-year-old Patti, signed by the French Opera as a novelty, achieved a sensational success. Patti was originally to sing three or four times, but before she sailed for England and European fame she sang no fewer than forty performances of eight different operas.

Native New Orleanians have achieved international acclaim in the music world, notably Louis Moreau Gottschalk, Ernest Guiraud, and Louis ("Satchmo") Armstrong, one of the all-time great jazz trumpeters. Gottschalk, a child prodigy who played the piano, was born in 1829. At thirteen he went to Paris to study and, still in his teens, he became the first American concert artist to gain European recognition. Later, Gottschalk became a composer, using the folk melodies of Louisiana for many of his themes. Guiraud, who was born in 1837, had his opera *Le Roi David* performed at the Orleans Theater when he was fifteen. He went to Paris to study and became a close friend of Georges Bizet. Guiraud composed the music for the recitatives in *Carmen*, after Bizet's death. He also completed Offenbach's *The Tales of Hoffmann*, and spent his life in France as a teacher at the Paris Conservatory and as a composer of operas.

Opera singers Norman Treigle, Shirley Verret, Marguerite Piazza, Sidney Rayner, Charles Anthony, and Ruth Falcon are all native New Orleanians. In the jazz world Pete Fountain and Al Hirt, native sons of New Orleans, have won renown throughout the world.

New Orleans maintains an opera company and a symphony orchestra. The opera company, organized in the 1940s, presents a series of performances each year, bringing in stars from the Metropolitan in New York to head its cast. The New Orleans Philhar-

monic Symphony Orchestra, organized in 1935, performs in split seasons, taking a break to accommodate Mardi Gras. Besides its New Orleans seasons, the orchestra goes on tour to several eastern cities and other southern cities each year. It won wide recognition in Europe on its 1982 tour.

But the big thing in music in New Orleans is jazz, which evolved into its present form in the late nineteenth and early twentieth centuries. It was born of a fusion of the folk music of the Negroes with the more structured European music they encountered when brought to the New Orleans area as slaves. As slaves, they gathered in public squares on holidays to dance the bamboula, a picturesque and exciting dance which gave expression to their feelings. The Negroes linked music, their tribal tunes, to everyday life, both work and play, with rhythm and swing, necessary elements of the music that was to become known as ragtime and jazz. (It first was spelled jass.)

Actually, the fusion of the musical styles grew out of gatherings in Congo Square on North Rampart Street, now known as Beauregard Square, following the Civil War. Jazz historian Gunther Schuller explains how music helped the black man retain the remnants of his African heritage: "Since religion and therefore music, to a limited extent, were the first forms of expression allowed the Negro, his conversion to Christianity and more gradually to European musical concepts was inevitable, given his natural talent for acculturation. At the same time, the oppressive side of the white master's attitudes and the consequent social ostracization of the Negro from the white man's world caused the Negro to preserve these sanctioned forms of expression in his own characteristic ways."

Jazz became a popular music form in the period between 1895 and 1917, roughly paralleling the period when Storyville, New Orleans' designated red-light district, flourished. The word *jazz* had its beginnings as an obscene expression in the bawdy houses, but won respectability because of the novelty and exuberance of the music. Jazz was not exclusive to Storyville, however. Many of the jazz pioneers put together bands that played at parades, picnics,

The jazz funeral is a New Orleans tradition, with mourners marching to the cemetery—accompanied by a jazz band. The Historic New Orleans Collection.

private parties, and funerals. It gained wide exposure through such appearances and has maintained its popularity through the years. The jazz funeral remains popular with modern-day blacks.

While jazz evolved because of the black man's musical instincts, ironically a group of white men spread its fame nationally. In 1917 a New Orleans quintet known as the Original Dixieland Jazz Band made a record at the Victor studios in New York City. Up to that time, jazz was but an obscure folk music. The record won immediate popularity, and the bouncy beat and swing of jazz swept to fame.

From New Orleans, jazz moved to Memphis, Chicago, New York, and Kansas City. Jazz historian James Lincoln Collier says that at the time of World War I, jazz was indigenous to New Orleans and played by only a few hundred musicians; that by 1940

The statue of jazz immortal Louis ("Satchmo") Armstrong stands at the Rampart Street entrance to Armstrong Park. Photo by A. J. Meek.

it was known over the world and by 1960 it was an accepted and important musical form.

Satchmo (as he was popularly known) Armstrong and his trumpet popularized jazz over the world. Born on July 4, 1900, and resident of an orphanage when he was given a horn, he blew his way to recognition quickly. Satchmo was a disciple of Joseph ("King") Oliver, one of the early jazz greats. He stayed in New Orleans until 1923, when he left for greener pastures in New York, Chicago, and other centers of entertainment. He returned in 1949

Preservation Hall, 726 St. Peter Street, where old-style music is played by men who learned from some of the jazz immortals. The Historic New Orleans Collection.

to rule as King Zulu at Mardi Gras. He died on July 7, 1971, as the recognized king of his profession, leaving his widow and millions of fans. Jazz is said to have come of age with Armstrong, who set the stylistic trend of the music in 1928 with his recording of "West Indies Blues." He became the ambassador of jazz after King Oliver and Sidney Bechet faded from the scene. The early jazz masters included, besides Oliver and Bechet, Buddy Bolden, Bunk Johnson, Tom Brown, Pop Foster, and Jelly Roll Morton, all of whom developed into stars.

Hirt (who died on April 27, 1999, in New Orleans) and Fountain became celebrated musicians in the 1950s after making names for themselves in the entertainment capitals of the world. Hirt, with his trumpet, and Fountain, with his clarinet, captured popular fancy with their individualistic styles. However, neither Hirt nor Fountain has been considered a traditional jazz artist in the style of Oliver, Bechet, and Armstrong.

Other New Orleans musicians who have gained prominence nationally include Wynton Marsalis, a classical trumpet player who won a Grammy at age 21 and the first ever Pulitzer Prize for jazz in 1997; Harry Connick, Jr., a singer and pianist and also a Grammy winner; Branford Marsalis, a saxophonist, and Jason Marsalis, a jazz drummer. Mahalia Jackson won world recognition as a gospel singer.

Jazz can be heard at a number of Vieux Carré nightclubs today. The Dukes of Dixieland attract much attention, but old-time jazz enthusiasts flock to Preservation Hall at 726 St. Peter Street to hear some of the old-style music played by men who learned under some of the jazz immortals. Preservation Hall is just that— a nightclub dedicated to perpetuating the style of jazz that has made New Orleans and the music famous

C.L.D. and W.G.C.

BIBLIOGRAPHY

Brunn, H. O. *The Story of the Original Dixieland Jazz Band.* Baton Rouge, 1960.

Collier, James Lincoln. *The Making of Jazz.* Boston, 1978.

Kmen, Henry A. *Music in New Orleans: The Formative years, 1791–1841.* Baton Rouge, 1966.

Longstreet, Stephen. *Sportin' House.* Los Angeles, 1965.

Schuller, Gunther. *Early Jazz: Its Roots and Musical Development.* New York, 1968.

Williams, Martin. *Jazz Masters of New Orleans.* New York, 1967.

21.

 RESTAURANTS AND COOKING

La cuisine Nouvelle Orléans, unique in all the world. Lip-smacking proof that too many cooks don't have to spoil the broth. A product of Continental chefs, as well as generations of budget-stretching housewives. Nature's bounty.

If the Sieur de Bienville had been looking for a gastronomical paradise, he could not have picked a more promising spot on which to establish his capital. In the lakes and bayous and the nearby Gulf of Mexico were the ingredients for a gourmet's delight: shrimp, crabs, fish, crawfish, oysters, turtles. In the swamps and woods were birds and game. The rich alluvial soil and warm climate guaranteed mouth-watering crops for truck farmers.

From France, Spain, Germany, Ireland, Italy, and Yugoslavia came settlers and immigrants who brought European traditions into the kitchen. Creoles, of Louisiana as well as from the West Indies, added new-world touches to their memories of the Old Countries. From Canada, directly and indirectly, came the Acadians, with their flair for introducing a soupçon of this or a jigger of that to make eating an adventure. The American Indians identified the pungent herbs that could be gathered in the area. The African slaves had their own way with a saucepan. Even the Kaintocks, such as floated down the river in flatboats ør keelboats, had a finger in the pot, introducing Anglo-Saxon recipes. Where else is there to

Culinary traditions have created la cuisine Nouvelle Orléans. Most of the many ethnic groups coming to New Orleans have contributed to what is called Creole cooking. Illustration by John C. Chase.

be found such a combination of locally produced foods? In what other city has there been such a variety of culinary influences?

The universal adjective applied to New Orleans cooking is *creole*, and the connotation is accurate because the term applies to people of European stock who were born in the Americas and to products that are indigenous to the area. By this definition, creole meals are available in other parts of Louisiana, in coastal Mississippi, and even in Texas. The true New Orleans cuisine, however, is served only in one city.

The two original contributions of New Orleans to the pleasure of living in America have been its food and its jazz music. One, Dixieland jazz, has been a static art form, with the same tunes, the same toe-tapping beat, even some of the same practitioners who revived the music in the 1940s. Not so the other, the cooking, which has changed with the times. New Orleans chefs and the cooks at home responded to the nouvelle cuisine of the 1970s, with its calorie-conscious emphasis on lightness. In one restaurant, Commander's Palace, even the traditional roux—a mixture of flour and shortening, with which many recipes began—has been largely abandoned in favor of stocks that are just as flavorful, and less fattening. Diners can taste no difference. La cuisine Nouvelle Orléans is a dynamic art.

Most visitors, of course, get their first sample of the palate-pleasing fare at one of the scores of restaurants that make up a major New Orleans industry. The eating places range from the internationally acclaimed houses dating back to the nineteenth century to the neighborhood cafes patronized by knowledgeable natives, from ethnic establishments to fast-food stands, from seafood havens where a diner's satisfaction is measured by the mound of crab shells piled up on the table before him to the po-boy emporia where overflow crowds mean it's noontime. Read on to learn what a po-boy is.

The food's the thing. Snow-white napery and gleaming goblets adorn the tables at the old-line places, of course, but the surroundings are not spectacular; the atmosphere is muted. The decor at the oldest restaurant, Antoine's, consists of photographs, newspaper clippings, and old menus. Dining out in New Orleans can be compared to an evening at the theater, but the scenery is secondary, the spotlight is on the cast and the chef's production.

The oldest eating place to be recorded in the city's annals was the Café des Emigrés, at which refugees from West Indian uprisings gathered as long ago as 1791. By 1820 the dining room of the Tremoulet Hotel was attracting attention. The hotel faced the Place d'Armes, before the construction of the Pontalba Buildings. In the 1830s the opening of the St. Charles, the St. Louis, and the Verandah hotels gave the families of southern plantation owners an opportunity to visit New Orleans and dine in the grand manner. At the St. Louis, which dated from 1837, the first free lunch was served to bibbers who came in for a noontime potion (not necessarily the first drink of the day in a town noted for its guzzling). The idea caught on, and the competition forced bar owners to lay out elaborate buffets at which customers could take their pick, without charge. He who drank could eat, a full meal if he wanted to go the route from soup to dessert. The custom did not die out until the twentieth century.

In 1840 a young man from Marseilles opened a boardinghouse, or *pension*, in the French Quarter. His name was Antoine Alciatore, and his establishment became Antoine's Restaurant, which has been operated ever since by his descendants. Here originated Oysters Rockefeller, so named because of their richness, and Pompano en Papillote, fish cooked in a paper bag. Here presidents and kings have dined. During his period in the White House, Richard M. Nixon lunched at Antoine's and recalled that he had taken his bride there on their honeymoon. And here occurred a never-to-be-forgotten New Orleans incident. President Franklin D. Roosevelt was taken to the restaurant for lunch. The city's mayor, Robert S. Maestri, a native son who spoke the New Orleans dialect, was at a loss for words in the presence of the patrician visitor. Finally he turned to the guest and asked: "How'd ja like them ersters, Mr. President?"

In 1863, during the Civil War, Louis Dutrey opened on Decatur Street a coffeehouse, which he operated with the help of his wife,

Luncheon for Franklin Roosevelt at Antoine's, 1937. Seated next to FDR are (*left*) Governor Richard W. Leche and (*right*) Mayor Robert S. Maestri. The Historic New Orleans Collection.

the former Elisabeth Kettenring. After Dutrey's death, the widow married Hypolite Bégue, a butcher who had been employed in the French Market across the street. The establishment began to offer elaborate mid-morning breakfasts to the vendors in the market. In 1880 the name was changed to Bégue's, and the culinary genius of Madame Bégue is immortalized in New Orleans lore. A restaurant in the Royal Sonesta Hotel has borrowed the name.

In the later years of the nineteenth century restaurants flourished. It was a time soon after slaves had been emancipated, but women hadn't. Wives and daughters were circumspect about their appearances in public, and the better restaurants maintained separate ladies' rooms in which female guests were seated. During Carnival week the code was relaxed, and women could be seen in the rooms that were part of the saloon areas. Popular restaurants during the period included Moreau's, on Canal Street, and Fabacher's, at Royal and Custom House (now Iberville) streets. In 1890 Emile Commander opened the establishment that bears his name, at Washington Avenue and Coliseum Street.

Until the early 1980s, it was owner-families rather than individual chefs who carried on the tradition of New Orleans restaurants and influenced their evolution. The descendants of Antoine Alciatore—Alciatores and Gustes—even have enhanced the image of the venerable eating house at 713 St. Louis Street. Galatoire's Restaurant, at 209 Bourbon Street, was purchased by Jean Galatoire in 1905—seventy-five years after a café was opened there by Victor Bero and has been carried on since by members of the Galatoire and Gooch families. In 1911, Anthony LaFranca opened Delmonico's in a building at 1300 St. Charles Avenue that had been a dairy store and ice cream parlor since about 1890. His wife, Marie, trained the chefs; some still were preparing the food when she died in 1975 and the place was taken over by their daughters, Angie Brown and Rose Dietrich, who sold the restaurant in 1998 to chef Emeril Lagasse. (Lagasse retained "Delmonico" as the restaurant's name, but he raised the luxury level of the decor and menu considerably.) A French champagne salesman, Arnaud Cazenave, opened Arnaud's, 813 Bienville Street, in 1920. It thrived with the food of a New Orleans rarity, a woman chef, Madame Pierre. After Cazenave's death, his daughter, Germaine Cazenave Wells, a singer, operated the establishment until she sold it to outside interests in the 1970s.

With the acquisition in 1946 of the Vieux Carré Restaurant, at Bourbon and Bienville, the Brennan family dynasty was launched. From this beginning, Owen Brennan and his sister, Ella Brennan Martin, planned to move the restaurant to its present location, 417 Royal Street. Owen Brennan died just before the move, but Brennan's is still operated by family members. The other branch of the family, headed by Ella Brennan Martin and her sister Dottie Brennan, owns Commander's Palace, in the Garden District. Other members of the extended Brennan Family operate numerous restaurants in and near the French Quarter—Mr. B's Bistro, at 201 Royal Street; Dickie Brennan's Steakhouse, at 716 Iberville Street; Palace Café, at 605 Canal Street; Bacco, at 310 Chartres Street; and Ralph Brennan's Red Fish Grill, at 115 Bourbon Street.

Lysle Aschaffenburg decided in 1947 that his elegant residential hotel, the Pontchartrain, should have distinguished dining facilities for its guests, and thus the Caribbean Room came into being to take its place among the storied New Orleans restaurants. The heirs of Pascal Radosta continue to run another of the premier New Orleans restaurants, Pascal's Manale, at 1838 Napoleon Avenue.

With the emergence of Louisiana-born Paul Prudhomme in the early 1980s, restaurant chefs began sharing the spotlight with New Orleans' legendary restaurant families. Prudhomme's restaurant, K-Paul's Louisiana Kitchen, at 416 Chartres Street, introduced the now-famous "blackening" technique in preparing fish and meat. Prudhomme's innovative cooking style has since had a profound effect on Creole and Acadian cuisine, challenging other restaurant chefs in south Louisiana to improvise on traditional ingredients, techniques, and dishes, and heralding the era of the "celebrity chef."

In 1990 Emeril Lagasse left Commander's Palace to strike out on his own with Emeril's restaurant, at 800 Tchoupitoulas Street in the Warehouse District. Lagasse's subsequent rise in the nation's culinary world was meteoric, and he now owns three restaurants in New Orleans (NOLA, at 534 St. Louis Street, as well as Delmonico and Emeril's), two in Las Vegas, Nevada (Emeril's New Orleans Fish House and Delmonico Steakhouse), and a sixth (Emeril's) in Orlando, Florida. Lagasse's fame has since multiplied with his hit television show *Emeril Live* on cable television's Food Network.

Other New Orleans chefs have found great success in opening their own restaurants, among them Susan Spicer (Bayona, at 430 Dauphine Street), Frank Brigtsen (Brigtsen's, at 723 Dante Street in the Carrollton Section), and Greg Sonnier (Gabrielle, at 3201 Esplanade Avenue).

This turn of events has brought a huge diversity to the city's distinctive cooking style, although its identifying characteristics—deep, rich flavors from traditional spices and herbs—have largely remained intact.

Any resident can rattle off a list of a dozen or two hotel dining rooms, neighborhood cafes, seafood houses, cafeterias, sandwich shops, delicatessens, and lunchrooms where the food has the unique flavor of la cuisine Nouvelle Orléans. Ask any taxicab driver, bellhop, clerk, policeman, or man on the street. New Orleanians keep up with such things.

Chefs' creations are not the entire menu. Every Monday in countless New Orleans homes, and many restaurants as well, red beans and rice has its day. The dish is available the rest of the week, too, but people like to taper off from a rich weekend with something that will stick to the ribs, as the saying goes. Kidney beans seasoned lavishly are served on steamed rice and generous portions of ham, hot sausage, or pickled pork, and everybody comes back for seconds. The dish has a long tradition in the Creole cuisine, and it is believed to be a Spanish contribution to the culinary arts of New Orleans.

The poor boy—it rhymes in New Orleans with "oh, joy"—is a product of hard times. There was an era in the 1920s and 1930s when a dime would buy one of the sandwiches, which was almost the equivalent of a full meal. They're more expensive now, but still nutritious, and inviting. Take a small loaf of French bread, or half of a large loaf. Split it down the middle. Dip the noncrust side of each half into hot beef gravy. Pile on slices of roast beef, ham, lettuce, pickles, tomatoes. Slap the halves together, open the mouth wide—and watch out for the gravy on the tie.

Despite the temptations, the average New Orleanian does not gorge himself, unless he goes to a crab boil, shrimp boil, or crawfish boil. Then he loosens his belt and forgets the consequences. The shellfish are boiled in water highly seasoned with a prepared mix. There's a knack to sucking the tender tidbits out of the crabs or crawfish, but any native-born New Orleanian knows how to get at the meat without wasted motion.

Restaurant critics and food historians Rima and Richard Collin have written that the Creole cuisine became fashionable upon the publication in 1885 of the *Christian Women's Exchange Creole Cookery Book* and Lafcadio Hearn's *La Cuisine Créole.* Another milestone, they said, was the appearance in 1900 of *The Picayune Creole Cook Book.* But they note that there are few rigid rules to govern the cook. In New Orleans, instinct comes into play.

J . W .

BIBLIOGRAPHY

Collin, Rima, and Richard Collin. *New Orleans Cookbook.* New York, 1979.
Land, Mary. *New Orleans Cuisine.* Cranbury, N.J., 1969.
Stanforth, Deirdre. *The New Orleans Restaurant Cookbook.* Garden City, 1967.

Note: The original authors are indebted to Gene Bourg, retired restaurant critic for the *Times-Picayune* and now contributor to national food publications, for updating this article.

22.

⚜ LITERATURE ⚜

The Americanization of Creole New Orleans is no better demonstrated than in the literature produced by New Orleanians during its nearly three centuries of existence. It is a far cry from the neoclassic bombast of Julien Poydras' French poems, extravagantly praising the dashing young Spanish governor Bernardo de Galvez, to John Kennedy Toole's Pulitzer Prize novel, *A Confederacy of Dunces,* with its realistic portrayal of earthy New Orleans.

Poydras, who lived in New Orleans and on his plantation in Pointe Coupée Parish, published in pamphlet form in 1777 *Épître à Don Bernard de Galvez* and *Le Dieu et les Nayades du Fleuve St. Louis.* Then two years later, Poydras produced *Le Prise du Morne du Baton Rouge,* describing Galvez's capture of the capital of West Florida from the English. These adulatory salutes to Galvez were the first pieces of literature written and published in New Orleans.

From Poydras' day to the Civil War, the literature of New Orleans was essentially in the French language and it was largely inspired by French romanticism. This was particularly true of Dominique and Adrien Rouquette, brothers who had studied in France in the 1830s. The poets were introduced into the circle of Chateaubriand, Lamartine, and Victor Hugo and they returned home, thoroughly steeped in romanticism. Adrien, in addition to his poems, wrote a prose Indian idyll, *La Nouvelle Atala*, after he had become a priest and missionary to the Choctaw Indians.

There were New Orleans French-language novelists in the nineteenth century, outstanding among whom was Dr. Alfred Mercier. A decade and a half before the Civil War, in 1845, the first anthology of Negro poetry in America was produced by a gifted group of free people of color. *Les Cenelles* contained eighty-two poems by seventeen poets. New Orleans–born Victor Sejour, a free person of color, became a successful playwright after settling in Paris, and more than thirty of his plays reached the French stage.

While French was the dominant language of literature produced in New Orleans up to the Civil War, the language was already in decline in Louisiana. And it was perhaps inevitable that from that time on, the writers of English books and stories should emerge. This emergence came during the vogue of regionalism in American literature. The first New Orleanian to win a national reputation was George Washington Cable, who wrote novels and short stories about the Creoles. Cable's *Old Creole Days*, *The Grandissimes*, and other pieces of fiction angered the Creoles, who felt Cable was ridiculing them.

Grace King, who became a great southern lady of letters, was very young both in age and as a writer, but she nurtured a warm feeling of sympathy for the Creoles, many of whose families had been ruined by the Civil War. Accordingly, she set out to portray the Creoles in a manner different from Cable's and she became the champion of these once distinguished people who had become the "new poor." Representative of her works are *Balcony Stories*, *Monsieur Motte*, *Tales of a Time and Place*, and the excellent *New Orleans: The Place and the People*.

Kate Chopin, who lived in New Orleans for a while, was a pioneer in the use of realism in her short stories and novels. Typical of this was *The Awakening*, a story of extramarital love, which created a furor when first published in 1899. She died in 1904 at the age of fifty-three, leaving a highly regarded collection of works.

Another lady of letters, who wrote many short stories and novels about the Creoles and New Orleans, was Ruth McEnery Stuart. Other women novelists who gained national reputations include Fanny Heaslip Lea, Gwen Bristow, and Shirley Ann Grau, whose

Mark Twain frequently visited George Washington Cable's home on Eighth Street, between Chestnut and Coliseum, and once they went on a lecture tour together. The two often met in lively discussion with other noted literary persons of the era. The Historic New Orleans Collection.

Lillian Hellman. Courtesy the *Times-Picayune/States-Item*.

Keepers of the House was awarded the Pulitzer Prize for fiction in 1965. Secure in a place among America's most distinguished playwrights is New Orleans–born Lillian Hellman, among whose many outstanding plays are *The Children's Hour*, *The Little Foxes*, and *Watch on the Rhine*.

New Orleans writers, native or by adoption, who were recognized nationally include Lyle Saxon, Hermann B. Deutsch, Harnett T. Kane, Thomas Sancton, E. P. O'Donnell, Robert Tallant, Hodding Carter, Frances Parkinson Keyes, Truman Capote, J. Hamilton Basso, and Roark Bradford. It was Bradford's *Ol' Man Adam an' His Chillun* that Marc Connelly turned into a Pulitzer Prize–winner, *The Green Pastures*, a long-running Broadway hit.

Many New Orleans writers, some already listed, began their careers as newspapermen. The old *Item* was particularly rich in talent. It is said that William S. Porter, while a reporter on the *Item*, adopted the name O. Henry, under which he became famous as a master of the surprise-ending short story. The story—true or imaginary?—goes that while quenching his thirst one day with some associates in a barroom near the paper, he commented that he wanted a pen name for his short stories. At that moment, someone called to the bartender: "Oh, Henry! Another of the same." A drinking mate immediately said: "There's your pseudonym," and William S. Porter became O. Henry for literary purposes.

Several decades and more before O. Henry, the *Item* gave employment to a young reporter from Cincinnati. His name was Lafcadio Hearn, whose beautifully chiseled prose caused someone to call him "a lapidary in words." Hearn's *Chita* is one of the classics not only of Louisiana literature but of American literature as well. Recognized writers who served apprenticeships on the *Item* include Marquis James, Pulitzer Prize biographer; Carl Carmer, historian and folklorist; Eugene Jolas, avant-garde French poet; and a number of others whose names have already been mentioned: Harnett Kane, Hodding Carter, Hamilton Basso, Thomas Sancton, and Hermann B. Deutsch.

From Walt Whitman to Tennessee Williams, New Orleans, but especially its French Quarter, has appealed to writers. Samuel Clemens first used his pen name Mark Twain in an article written for the *Crescent*, a newspaper. During the 1920s, the French Quarter was a rendezvous for writers, a sort of "branch office" for Paris' Left Bank. James Feibleman, who later held a chair of philosophy at Tulane University, but then a budding young poet, wrote of that long ago: "The French Quarter furnished the kind of sensually pleasant and socially tolerant atmosphere which artists have sought and found in the Paris of Montparnasse and New York of Greenwich Village. . . . There were few night clubs in the Quarter in those days, but mostly it was given over to an assortment of people moving quietly, rich people and poor, happy to be left alone just to be by themselves."

Such was the atmosphere which attracted Sherwood Anderson, William Faulkner, Oliver La Farge, Bill Spratling, and others to the French Quarter, and they often hosted such visiting writers as Gertrude Stein, John Steinbeck, Herbert Asbury, Erskine Caldwell, and John Dos Passos, among others. The same literary climate and literary coterie spawned the *Double Dealer*, one of the "little" magazines which merited and won so much respect in the 1920s. In the *Double Dealer* appeared some of the early work of Faulkner, Hemingway, and Thornton Wilder.

The French Quarter, with its Bohemian atmosphere and plethora of bars, maintained its attraction for writers into the twenty-first century. As the previous century wound down, Richard Ford, a resident of the Quarter at the time, won a Pulitzer Prize for his novel *Independence Day*. Stephen Ambrose, a professor at the University of New Orleans, won national recognition for his biographies of Dwight Eisenhower and Richard Nixon, as well as for *Citizen Soldiers: The Victors* and *Undaunted Courage: Meriwether Lewis, Thomas Jefferson, and the Opening of the American West*. And Anne Rice, a prolific writer of novels of the supernatural, became New Orleans' best-selling novelist.

The list of New Orleans writers so impressed Susan Larson, the book-page editor of the *Times-Picayune,* that she wrote a book about them, *The Booklover's Guide to New Orleans*, which was published by LSU Press in 1999.

This chapter opened with a reference to John Kennedy Toole's *A Confederacy of Dunces,* which found its way into print only because a great Louisiana writer, not a New Orleanian, urged the Louisiana State University Press to publish it. Walker Percy is thus the godfather of Toole's posthumous prize-winning bestseller, which during the young author's life was submitted to only one publisher, without success. After his death, his mother sent the

Tennessee Williams. Courtesy the *Times-Picayune/States-Item*.

manuscript to a number of publishers. All rejected it. The Pulitzer Prize Committee's choice of *A Confederacy of Dunces* justified the judgment of Walker Percy and the confidence of the LSU Press that John Kennedy Toole had produced a masterpiece.

New Orleans newspapers won Pulitzer Prizes—the *States* in 1951 and the *Times-Picayune* in 1997. The 1951 prize was for a series of editorials in the New Orleans *States* titled "Government by Treaty," which attacked the human rights covenant of the United Nations, and two 1997 awards were for editorial cartoons and a series on depletion of the world's fisheries.

C.L.D. and W.G.C.

BIBLIOGRAPHY

Dufour, Charles L. *Ten Flags in the Wind.* New York, 1967.
Durno, A. G. "Literature and Art." In *Standard History of New Orleans,* ed. Henry Rightor. New York, 1900.

23.

✤ ART ✤

Painters at Jackson Square almost outnumber the pigeons. They hang their French Quarter scenes on the iron fences that enclose the old Place d'Armes. They set up their easels on the sidewalk and produce, in crayon or charcoal, instant portraits for tourists.

Many of these Jackson Square artists, although not natives, make New Orleans their home and around the calendar they are on hand to make a sale or do a portrait. Many others "hibernate" in the Vieux Carré, coming with their colors and brushes to New Orleans for the duration of the tourist season.

Few places in the country offer the picturesque attractiveness of the Vieux Carré with its cool courtyards, quaint buildings, lacelike ironwork, and nostalgia. Visitors who have been to Paris see in Jackson Square and its art colony another Place du Tertre of Montmartre fame.

The artists who flock to New Orleans year after year during the fall and winter seasons are following a tradition that goes back to the period 1815–1830, and perhaps even farther. It was to that period that Dr. Isaac M. Cline, art collector, dealer, and critic, referred when he wrote: "New Orleans was the Mecca of American artists."

The list of important painters who visited New Orleans in the first half of the nineteenth century is impressive, and there are hundreds of family portraits in existence from their brushes.

Among these artists was John James Audubon (1785 – 1851), who was in and out of New Orleans from 1821 to 1826 preparing preliminary sketches for his fabulous *Birds of America*. John Wesley Jarvis (1780 – 1840) wintered in New Orleans from 1816 to 1834, painting portraits and miniatures. Apprenticed to Jarvis was Henry Inman (1801 – 1846), who established a reputation as a portraitist. Samuel F. B. Morse (1791 – 1872) won so much fame as inventor of the telegraph that his stature as a painter has been much obscured. Morse painted in New Orleans on visits between 1816 and 1820. Also active during the first half of the nineteenth century in New Orleans were George Catlin (1796 – 1872), who later won fame as a painter of Indians; Louis Antoine Collas (1775 – ?); G. P. A. Healy (1813 – 1894); Matthew H. Jouett (1787 – 1827), a pupil of Gilbert Stuart; Charles Alexandre Lesueur (1778 – 1846), a gifted water-color painter; Thomas Sully (1783 – 1872);

Paintings hanging on the iron fences in Jackson Square can be purchased from the artist, or you can have your portrait done in crayon or charcoal. Photo by A. J. Meek.

Jean Joseph Vaudechamp (1790–1866); John Vanderlyn (1775–1852); Dominique Canova (1800–1865); Benjamin H. B. Latrobe (1764–1820), whose versatility included art as well as architecture; Francisco Salazar (1785–1830); Jacques Amans (1801–1888); and many others.

The second half of the nineteenth century also brought distinguished artists to New Orleans. The most famous of these were Edgar Degas, French impressionist, and George Inness (1825–1894), one of the world's great landscape painters. Degas visited relatives here for about four months in the winter of 1872–1873, and a painting in the collection of the New Orleans Museum of Art in City Park is a reminder of the most noteworthy artistic event ever to occur in New Orleans. While here, Degas produced a portrait of his cousin, Estelle Musson. The oil was purchased in 1965 for $190,000, which was raised by popular subscription. Another work done during Degas' visit, *The Cotton Office in New Orleans*, hangs in the museum in Pau, France. It has been called the most significant painting ever produced by a foreign artist in America. During his New Orleans visit, Degas resided with relatives, the Musson family, at 2306 Esplanade Avenue. George Inness worked in New Orleans in the late 1880s and early 1890s.

Other distinguished artists who painted in New Orleans after the Civil War include Andres Molinary (1847–1915); Paul Poincy (1833–1909); Richard Clague (1821–1873); Adrien Persac (1823–1873); Leon Pomarede (1807–1892); William Aiken Walker (1838–1921); William H. Buck (1840–1888); and Bror A. Wikstrom (1854–1909), who produced not only landscape, marine, and genre paintings of merit but the designs of Carnival parades as well.

Art in New Orleans was given a forceful stimulus with the arrival from New England of two brothers, Ellsworth Woodward (1861–1939) and William Woodward (1859–1939), in the mid-1880s. Both were painters, engravers, and art educators and both affiliated themselves with the H. Sophie Newcomb College, the women's division of Tulane University. Ellsworth Woodward, who was director of the Newcomb Art School, and his brother,

While in New Orleans in 1872, Edgar Degas painted this portrait of his cousin Estelle Musson Degas. It was purchased in 1965 by the New Orleans Museum of Art with funds raised by subscription. Courtesy of New Orleans Museum of Art.

assisted by Mary Given Sheerer and Joseph Fortune Meyer, combined their talents and enthusiasm to establish the Newcomb Pottery, which won international acclaim as the twentieth century was dawning. They mixed clay from St. Tammany Parish—across Lake Pontchartrain from New Orleans—with silt filtered from the waters of the Mississippi River, and produced a glaze and tints that captured a bronze medal at the Paris Exposition of 1900. Newcomb Pottery pieces are collectors' items.

Twentieth-century artists based in New Orleans, many of whom specialized in New Orleans scenes, included the Woodward brothers, Selina Bres Gregory, Alexander Drysdale, George F. Castledon, Boyd Cruise, Charles Bein, Knute Heldner, John McCrady, Clarence Millet, Charles Reinike, Nell Pomeroy O'Brien, Ida Kohlmyer, Caroline Wogan Durieux, Morris Henry Hobbs, and, among others, Dr. Marion Souchon, a noted physician who in his later years turned with amazing success to painting primitives.

In sculpture, New Orleans has been quite productive. The first local sculptor to win recognition was Eugene Warburg (1825–1859), a free person of color who continued his studies and work in Italy in the early 1850s. Italian-born Achille Perelli (1822–1891) was active as both a sculptor and painter. Angela Gregory, a pupil of Bourdelle, Rai Grainer Murray, Lin Emery, and Enrique Alferez established excellent reputations as sculptors after World War II.

The fence around Jackson Square is not the only place where paintings of New Orleans may be found. In the numerous galleries along Royal, Chartres, and Decatur streets and the cross streets of the Vieux Carré are more substantial, and costlier, works by local artists, some well established, some seeking recognition. There are also galleries interspersed among the antique shops and second-hand furniture stores on Magazine Street in the Uptown section of the city.

The New Orleans art scene, traditionally alive with treasured exhibits at the New Orleans Museum of Art, has been enhanced by the opening of the Ogden Museum of Southern Art, in which the works of great southern artists are shown. The new museum is located at Lee Circle, while NOMA remains in picturesque City Park.

Another adjunct to the art community is the Contemporary Arts Center on Camp Street, near the Ogden Museum.

C.L.D. and J.W.

BIBLIOGRAPHY

Cline, Isaac M. *Contemporary Art and Artists in New Orleans.* New Orleans, 1924.

Durno, A. G. "Literature and Art." In *Standard History of New Orleans,* ed. Henry Rightor. New York, 1900.

Thompson, N. Ruth Farr. "A Biographical Checklist of Artists in New Orleans in the Nineteenth Century." M.A. thesis, LSU, 1970.

24.

New Orleans is the sum total of the many peoples who have inhabited it since Jean-Baptiste Le Moyne, Sieur de Bienville, founded the city in 1718. By the same token the city is the sum total of certain specific individuals among this multiplicity of peoples whose contributions have made New Orleans what it is. Among these individuals of many nations are the following:

René Robert Cavelier, Sieur de La Salle (1643–1687), descended the Mississippi to the Gulf of Mexico in 1682 and on April 9 claimed all the land drained by the great river and its tributaries for Louis XIV of France, in whose honor he called Louisiane the vast territory between the Rockies and the Alleghenies. His second expedition to settle Louisiana failed when he was murdered by his own men in 1687.

Pierre Le Moyne, Sieur d'Iberville (1661–1706), rediscovered the Mississippi River in 1699 and began the settlement of Louisiana, first at Biloxi (now Ocean Springs, Mississippi) and later Mobile. Iberville, of a famous French Canadian family, won fame as a soldier, sailor, and explorer and was known as the Canadian Cid. He died in Havana of yellow fever, while campaigning against the English.

Jean-Baptiste Le Moyne, Sieur de Bienville (1680–1768), who accompanied his brother, Iberville, to Louisiana at the age of nineteen, was the founder of New Orleans in 1718. For more than four decades he served France in Louisiana in positions of command, sometimes as governor of the colony. He died in Paris in a house on the rue Vivienne, now marked by a plaque.

John Law (1671–1729), a mathematical and financial wizard, organized a bank, invented paper money, and established the Company of the West to settle and exploit Louisiana. It was the Scotsman Law who ordered the founding of New Orleans, which he named for his friend Philippe, duc d'Orléans, the regent for the child king, Louis XV. Law bankrupted France, but he settled Louisiana.

Antonio de Ulloa (1716–1795) was the first Spanish governor of Louisiana. Although a distinguished naval officer and a brilliant scientist, he was devoid of talents as an administrator and his relations with the Creoles went from bad to worse, sparking a bloodless revolution in 1768. The Creoles expelled Ulloa in this, the first revolution in the Americas against a European monarch.

Alexander O'Reilly (1725–1794), Irishman turned Spanish general, came to New Orleans in 1769 at the head of 2,600 troops to suppress the revolution. Because, on orders of the Spanish Crown, he tried the leaders of the conspiracy and executed five of them, history has unjustly called him "Bloody" O'Reilly. In fact, he was just, mild, and able and he firmly established Spain in Louisiana.

Bernardo de Galvez (1746–1786) was governor of Louisiana during the American Revolution, and his administration was marked by his aid to the Americans in supplying arms, powder, and ammunition through the American agent, Oliver Pollock. Other significant events in Galvez's regime were the capture from the British of Manchac, Baton Rouge, and Natchez (1779), Mobile (1780), and Pensacola (1781).

de Galvez

Oliver Pollock (1737–1823), Irish-born American merchant in New Orleans, was granted privileges by Spanish authorities for making flour available to O'Reilly at a fair price. As agent for the Continental Congress and Virginia, Pollock pledged his fortune in the American cause as he induced Galvez to aid the colonists in their struggle with England. No one contributed more financially than did Pollock.

Oliver Pollock

Don Andrés Almonester y Roxas (1725–1798) came to New Orleans in 1770 as royal notary and received other official appointments from Spanish Governor Unzaga, all of which led to fame and fortune. After the fire of 1788, Almonester supplied funds to rebuild St. Louis Cathedral and he advanced money for the building of the Cabildo. His daughter Micaela married Joseph Xavier Celestin de Pontalba.

Esteban Miró (1744–1795), Spanish governor of Louisiana from 1785 to 1791, was an able adminstrator. It was during Miró's regime—from 1782 to 1785, he was acting governor during Galvez's absence from Louisiana—that sixteen hundred Acadians were brought from France to Louisiana. This was the largest transatlantic migration in the entire American colonial period.

François Louis Hector, Baron de Carondelet (1748–1807), Belgian nobleman in the Spanish service, governed Louisiana from 1792 to 1797. Projects of far-reaching consequences came during his regime: the first theater opened; street lights were provided; the position of night watchman was created; a navigation canal to the lake was dug; the first newspaper, *Moniteur de la Louisiane*, was launched.

Pierre Clément de Laussat (1756–1835) was sent by Napoleon to Louisiana to prepare for the arrival of French occupying troops in 1803. When Napoleon changed his mind and sold Louisiana to the United States, Laussat remained to receive the colony from Spain on November 30, 1803, and to transfer it to the United States on December 20.

William Charles Coles Claiborne (1775–1817), Virginia-born governor of Mississippi Territory, with General James Wilkinson received Louisiana from France on December 20, 1803. President Jefferson appointed him governor of Orleans Territory (present Louisiana) and when it became a state in 1812, Claiborne was its first elected governor. In 1816, he was elected senator but died before taking his seat.

James H. Caldwell (1793–1863), an English actor, became New Orleans' first important promoter. He built the first American Theater on Camp Street and later the famous St. Charles Theater; he started a gas company, whose lineal "descendant" exists today; he was a real estate developer; and he became a successful politician.

Samuel Jarvis Peters (1801–1855), a promoter and real estate speculator, headed with Caldwell a syndicate of Americans, which developed New Orleans above Canal Street, paving the way for the upriver growth of the city.

Bernard de Marigny (1785–1868), a fabulous member of a Creole family long established in Louisiana, was a compulsive gambler, who imported crap shooting to New Orleans to his own financial disaster. Though reduced from great wealth to poverty he remained for half a century one of the city's most picturesque characters.

Etienne Boré (1741–1820) was Louisiana's "Father of the Sugar Industry." Although far from being the first to granulate sugar, Boré was the first to plant it on a large scale, and when his 1796 crop brought in $12,000, with a profit of $5,000, the sugar industry in Louisiana was born. Laussat appointed him mayor of New Orleans during the brief French regime in 1803.

Daniel Clark (1766–1813), wealthy Irish-born merchant, plantation owner, and land investor, served as United States consul at New Orleans during the Spanish regime. He hoped to be named governor and was bitter when Claiborne got the appointment. Clark was mixed up with Aaron Burr. Clark's daughter, Myra Clark

Gaines, was in litigation for more than half a century to prove she was his legitimate heir.

John James Audubon (1785–1851), noted naturalist and painter, lived for a while in New Orleans, where he hunted and studied many of the specimens that he later drew and painted for his monumental work, *Birds of America*.

Jean Laffite (1780?–1826?) and his brother Pierre have traditionally been called pirates, but they were in fact smugglers, especially involved in the illicit importation of slaves, which they sold by the pound at their Barataria headquarters on the Gulf of Mexico. The Laffite brothers supplied General Andrew Jackson with flints for his muskets, but neither was on the Chalmette battlefield on January 8, 1815.

Norbert Rillieux (1806–1894), a free person of color, was sent to France by his white father to complete his education. He had a marked aptitude for physics, mechanics, and chemistry, and when he returned to New Orleans his experiments led to the development of an evaporation process which revolutionized the manufacture of sugar.

Baroness Pontalba (1795–1874), born Micaela Almonester, built the two stately Pontalba Buildings that flank Jackson Square. These were row houses under a single roof and not, as often erroneously stated, the first apartment houses in the United States. Each building had sixteen separate dwellings. By February, 1851, they were completed.

The greatest benefactors of New Orleans in the nineteenth century were all crusty old bachelors, often accused of being miserly. These were *John McDonogh* (1779–1850), who left a fortune for public schools; *Judah Touro* (1775–1854), a Jewish philanthropist who contributed to all faiths; *Alexander Milne* (1742–1836), whose bequest established homes for needy children; and *Paul Tulane* (1801–1887), the founder of Tulane University.

Paul Morphy (1837–1884) was the greatest chess player of his day, enjoying an international reputation in the mid-nineteenth century.

James Gallier (1798–1866) and son of the same name (1827–1868) were famous nineteenth-century architects. Gallier, Sr., a specialist in the Greek Revival, built old City Hall and many homes still standing in New Orleans. Gallier, Jr., built the famous French Opera House, destroyed by fire in 1919.

Pierre Gustave Toutant Beauregard (1818–1893), a West Point graduate, distinguished himself in the Mexican War. He joined the Confederacy in 1861 and opened the Civil War with the capture of Fort Sumter.

Judah P. Benjamin (1811–1884), a New Orleans lawyer and U.S. senator, served successively as attorney general, secretary of war, and secretary of state in Jefferson Davis' Confederate cabinet. He was called the Brains of the Confederacy. After the collapse of the Confederacy, he escaped to England, where he had a distinguished career as a lawyer.

James B. Eads (1820–1887) was an American engineer. His system of jetties at the mouth of the Mississippi River kept the channel from silting up and thus isolating New Orleans as a world port. Eads undertook the project on a "no channel, no pay" agreement with the government. New Orleans' debt to Eads is a tremendous one.

Mrs. Josephine Louise LeMonnier Newcomb (1816–1901) endowed a college for women within the framework of Tulane University as a memorial to her daughter Harriott Sophie Newcomb. In 1886, Mrs. Newcomb's initial gift of $100,000, which was later augmented, launched Newcomb College.

The Gordon sisters, Jean (1867–1931) and Kate (1861–1932), were activists for the improvement of New Orleans and the betterment of the poor in the city. They were three-quarters of a century ahead of the women's lib movement in civic affairs.

Isaac Delgado (1839–1912) was a wealthy sugar planter. His bequests to the city of New Orleans included funds to establish an art gallery (Delgado Museum, now New Orleans Museum of Art) and a technical school (now Delgado College).

Rudolph Matas (1862–1957) was an internationally famed surgeon who was one of the pioneers in vascular surgery. He was among the first American physicians to support Dr. Carlos Finlay's thesis that yellow fever was transmitted by the stegomyia mosquito.

Alton Ochsner (1896–1981), celebrated surgeon and founder of the internationally famous hospital that bears his name, was among the first to relate tobacco smoking to lung cancer. He was also a specialist in vascular surgery.

Edgar Stern (1886–1959) and his wife, Edith Rosenwald Stern (1895–1980), contributed more to New Orleans than any other philanthropists. Among the many recipients of the Stern generosity were the New Orleans Philharmonic Symphony, the New Orleans Museum of Art, and Dillard University.

Louis Armstrong (1900–1971) won international fame as a jazz trumpeter. He learned to play at the age of thirteen while residing at a New Orleans boys' home, then played with noted jazz artists King Oliver and Kid Ory. Popularly known as Satchmo, Armstrong is credited with influencing Western popular music during a career which took him to Chicago, New York, and other U.S. cities, and to Europe. He starred in several motion pictures.

C.L.D.

25.

❧ WOMEN ❧

In the nineteenth century, the chief benefactors of New Orleans were all bachelors—John McDonogh, Alexander Milne, Judah Touro, Paul Tulane, for example—but in the twentieth century the movement for improvement and progress in the city was paced by a galaxy of women who were determined to do things and did them.

In the forefront of these dedicated ladies, who braved not only politicians, legislatures, civic groups, and community leaders, but tradition as well, were two sisters, Kate Gordon (1861–1932) and Jean Gordon (1867–1931). A close friend of the Gordon sisters summed up their contributions to New Orleans: "There is scarcely a phase of the history of the city for the past 40 years that could be adequately written without a mention of Jean Gordon."

One can only touch lightly on some of the wonderful things the Gordon sisters accomplished. They led the fight for modern drainage; established the first hospital for tubercular patients; won the right for women to attend Tulane University's medical school; sought the vote for women; established the first day nursery and the organization that became the Family Service Society; pushed for a child labor bill; developed the Milne home for feeble-minded girls. As one writer put it: "Each of these determined women had her own pet programs, but the sisters were mutually supporting in all of them. They dared everything, feared nobody and gave all of

Grace King. The Historic New Orleans Collection.

themselves to the causes for which they fought." Describing their
efforts, Kate Gordon once said: "The reason we've accomplished
what we have, Jean and I, is because we never cared what people
thought."

Grace King (1852–1932) became a distinguished woman of
letters and established herself as a historian of Louisiana and a teller

of picturesque New Orleans tales. Eliza Jane Poitevent (Mrs. A. W. Holbrook, later ·Mrs. George Nicholson) (1849–1896) became not only the first woman editor and publisher of a daily newspaper, the *Picayune*, but indulged in literature herself under the pen name Pearl Rivers. Despite her busy life, she found time for philanthropy. On her death, the rival newspaper, the *Times-Democrat*, noted that every worthy cause in New Orleans "found in Mrs. Nicholson an ardent sympathizer, a powerful helper with voice, money, labor, time and pen."

Sophie B. Wright (1866–1912) was an educator who did things despite having been crippled since childhood. She opened what is believed to be the first free night school in the country and pioneered adult education more than twenty years before the concept became the concern of educators.

Women philanthropists and activists who devoted themselves to the expansion of medical facilities in New Orleans included Mrs. Ida Richardson (1830–1910), who was especially concerned with Tulane's medical school; Dr. Sara T. Mayo, who in 1905 established the New Orleans Dispensary for Women and Children, which grew into the hospital that bore her name for many years; Mrs. Deborah Milliken, who provided funds to build and endow the Milliken Memorial Hospital for Children; and Mrs. John Dibert, whose many benefactions included such memorials to her husband as the Dibert Tuberculosis Hospital, a residence for the Sisters of Charity, the John Dibert School, and the Dibert Memorial Home for Women and Children.

In the last decade of the nineteenth century, significant social work among Italian immigrants was undertaken by Mother Cabrini—Saint Frances Xavier Cabrini—who pursued her works of mercy in New Orleans for several years. She was the first saint identified with the United States.

Kingsley House, 911 Market Street, is a monument to the memory of Eleanor McMain (1868–1934), another pioneer social worker in New Orleans, who espoused and worked tirelessly for social reform in Louisiana.

There were also Mrs. Olive A. Stallings (1860–1940), termed

Born Micaela Almonester in 1795, the Baroness Pontalba was responsible for the construction of the Pontalba Buildings that flank Jackson Square. They were completed by February, 1851. From the Collections of the Louisiana State Museum.

the "playground mother" of the city for having financed the first playground for children in New Orleans; Sister Stanislaus—born Katie Malone—whose humanitarian work at Charity Hospital spanned more than half a century; Elizabeth Werlein (1887–1946) and Mrs. J. Oscar Nixon (1857–1947), who led the campaign to rescue the Vieux Carré from slumdom. The list, almost endless, of those who worked for the civic, sociological, and cultural improvement of New Orleans includes Mrs. Julius Friend, Mrs. Charles F. Buck, Jr., Mrs. James W. Reily, Mrs. Roydon Douglas, Mrs. Ernest Robin, Mrs. Martha Robinson, and Mrs. Eunice Laird.

And then, of course, there is Margaret Gaffney Haughery, whose monument is reportedly the first in the United States—certainly among the first—to a woman. Margaret Haughery was an Irish immigrant who worked as a chambermaid in a hotel, saved money to buy a bakery, and then with her product and her profits befriended the poor of the city. When Margaret died, governors and mayors and distinguished citizens followed her cortege.

New Orleans women developed an interest in city politics as the twentieth century neared its end, with the result that Dorothy Mae Taylor, Peggy Wilson, Jacquelyn Clarkson, Suzanne Haik Terrell, and Ellen Hazeur won election to the City Council between 1986 and 1994.

Two New Orleans women won election to the United States Congress: Lindy (Mrs. Hale) Boggs to the House of Representatives and Mary Landrieu to the United States Senate. Mrs. Boggs succeeded her husband, Hale, who was lost in a plane accident in Alaska, and Mary Landrieu served two terms as state treasurer before being elected to the Senate.

A number of New Orleans women served in the state legislature in the latter part of the century, and one of them, Melinda Schwegmann, was lieutenant governor for one term. Suzanne Haik Terrell was elected state commissioner of elections after her stint on the council. Still other women became involved in the political system, serving as district judges and in several other offices.

Actually, the trailblazer among women in New Orleans political life is Jacqueline Leonhard, a former news reporter who won election to the Orleans Parish School Board in 1948 and served as its president from December 8, 1950, to early December of 1952.

C.L.D.

BIBLIOGRAPHY

Chase, John C., *et al. Citoyens, Progrés et Politique de la Nouvelle Orléans.* New Orleans, 1964.

26.

⚜ SPORTS ⚜

Sports records and championships are as much a part of New Orleans as its culture, cuisine, or commerce. As early as the 1830s, New Orleans was an established center for horse racing. Championship prizefights in the late nineteenth century and title events in football, basketball, baseball, and other sports were held throughout the twentieth century.

New Orleans has been the site of two world heavyweight championship fights, five Super Bowls, fifty Sugar Bowl games, several of which have decided national collegiate championships, the national tournament to decide the collegiate basketball champion, plus many other sports spectaculars. The city holds the nation's indoor crowd records for heavyweight championship fights and for professional and college basketball.

While the Sugar Bowl and the Superdome have grabbed the bulk of attention in recent years, in the 1890s the city's sports fame centered on the Carnival of Champions in prizefighting. On three successive nights, September 5–7, 1892, the Olympic Club at Royal and Montegut streets was the scene of championship bouts. George Dixon won the featherweight title and Jack McAuliffe retained his lightweight crown in the first two nights. In the main attraction, "Gentleman Jim" Corbett knocked out John L. Sullivan in the twenty-first round to win the heavyweight championship. Ten thousand people crowded into the gymnasium, where

ringside seats cost $100. The purse was $25,000, the gate totaled $62,068, and, it is said, spectators' wagers amounted to
$500,000.

New Orleans played the leading role in two earlier world championship fights, which, because of the law, had to be staged surrep-
titiously in Mississippi. At Mississippi City, on February 7, 1882,
in the first world heavyweight championship fight—a bare-
knuckle event—John L. Sullivan took thirty-two minutes and
eight rounds to knock out Paddy Ryan. Three thousand fight fans
from New Orleans went to the Gulf Coast site via train and boat.
Seven years later, on July 8, 1889, Sullivan knocked out Jake
Kilrain in seventy-four rounds in the last bare-knuckle championship fight at Richburg, Mississippi, a sawmill community near
Hattiesburg. Kilrain could not come out for the seventy-fifth
round. (The rounds were ended each time a fighter went down.)

Circumstances of the two fights were similar in that the promot-
ers had to secretly arrange locations to avoid the law. For the
Kilrain-Sullivan matchup, fans poured into New Orleans over the
Fourth of July weekend, buying tickets without knowing where
the bout would take place. Three trains were reserved to transport
the fans to the location, with the tickets marked only "Destination
and Return." Authorities, alerted to arrest Sullivan when he
reached New Orleans, were thwarted when he registered at the St.
Charles Hotel as W. J. Barnett. The subterfuge fooled no one, but
police had no orders to pick up a Barnett. The trains set out on the
morning of July 8 for an undisclosed location in Mississippi, whose
governor had posted a $1,000 reward for the arrest of Kilrain
and Sullivan. (Prizefighting was also illegal in Mississippi.) Approximately three thousand persons disembarked at the sawmill
site, where only hours before workmen had erected bleachers for
the event.

By the time the Sullivan-Corbett fight was arranged, Louisiana
had legalized prizefighting. The first title fight in New Orleans,
incidentally, was fought in 1891, when the original Jack Dempsey,
the "Nonpareil," lost his middleweight crown to Australian Robert Fitzsimmons. New Orleans and its environs produced world
champions in Pete Herman, bantamweight; Tony Canzoneri (of

Slidell) and Joe Brown, lightweights; and Willie Pastrano, light heavyweight.

The biggest boxing event of this century pitted Muhammad Ali against Leon Spinks in the Superdome in 1978 before a record indoor crowd of 63,000. Ali won back the title he had lost to Spinks, and collected $3.2 million. Spinks received $3.8 million. Both sums were records.

Tulane University, where football history dates from 1893, won Southern Conference championships or co-championships in 1925, 1929, 1930, and 1931, and Southeastern Conference titles in 1934, 1939, and 1949. The 1925 team turned down an invitation to the Rose Bowl, but the 1931 team accepted, losing to Southern California, 21-12. Stars of that team were two All-Americas, end Jerry Dalrymple and halfback Don Zimmerman. The 1934 team played in the first Sugar Bowl, defeating Temple, 20-14, and the 1939 team lost to Texas A & M 14-13 in the Sugar Bowl.

Through most of the twentieth century, Tulane and Louisiana State University engaged in one of the most intense rivalries in college football, but in the latter part of the century, enthusiasm for the match-up waned. LSU dominated the series for a twenty-four-year stretch. In 1973, when Tulane ended the streak, the game was viewed by 86,598 people, the largest crowd ever to witness a game in the South up to that time. LSU discontinued the annual rivalry during the 1990s, but resumed with a game in 2001. Games are also scheduled for 2005 and 2009. LSU gave the state something to cheer about in 1958, when the Tigers won the national championship with a team starring All-America Billy Cannon.

A postseason football game for New Orleans was first suggested by James M. Thomson, publisher of the *Item;* his sports editor, Fred Digby, sparked the campaign which made the game a reality. A success from the start, the Sugar Bowl brought about the eventual expansion of Tulane Stadium from 25,000 to 81,000 permanent seats. The Sugar Bowl games have attracted national attention through the years, and several have decided national championships. The games were played in Tulane Stadium until 1975, when they were moved to the Superdome. In 1981, Tulane Stadium was dismantled.

The success of the Sugar Bowl and New Orleans fans' enthusiastic reception of professional exhibition football games in the 1960s served as the catalyst in bringing a National Football League franchise to New Orleans in 1967. The team, the Saints, played in Tulane Stadium for seven years, then moved to the Superdome when it was completed in 1974. The Saints, advancing to the NFL playoffs twice, have won only one playoff game.

The Superdome, built at a cost of $163 million, runs up annual deficits but is considered a success because it spurs the local economy enormously. A multipurpose facility, it has a seating capacity of 76,000 for football, up to 60,000 for baseball and basketball, and as many as 95,000 when converted to an auditorium. It is financed by rental fees and a 4 percent hotel-motel tax.

Because it can accommodate such large crowds and is situated in the business district near the big hotels, the Superdome has been able to attract the Super Bowl frequently. The Superdome is also the site of the annual Sugar Bowl, which is now part of the rotation for college football's national championship game.

Minor league baseball was popular during the years the Pelicans played in the Southern Association. They existed from 1887 through 1959, winning the pennant thirteen times. Baseball was revived in New Orleans in 1993 with the Zephyrs, affiliated with the American Association at first, then later becoming a member of the Pacific Coast League when the minor leagues went through a realignment. The Zephyrs have prospered, encouraging their owners to enlist state aid to build a $25 million stadium on Airline Drive in Jefferson Parish.

In recent times women's sports, including basketball, hockey, and soccer, have become popular at New Orleans college campuses. Teams representing the University of New Orleans, Tulane, Loyola, Southern, Dillard, and Xavier draw enthusiastic crowds.

As long ago as the 1830s, horse racing was a favorite sport in New Orleans. Before the Civil War, there were five race tracks in and about the city. The most famous was the Metairie Race Course, where match races were staged between two famous horses, LeCompte and Lexington, in 1854. Kentucky-owned Lexington

Built at a cost of $163 million, the multipurpose Louisiana Superdome has been the
scene of world heavyweight boxing championship fights, Sugar Bowl games, several
Super Bowls, national collegiate basketball championships, and many other sports
spectaculars. Photo by Jack Beech.

nosed out LeCompte in the series, but Louisiana fans fell in love with
LeCompte, and the horse was buried at a stud farm near Alexandria.
In 1872 the Fair Grounds track was opened and continues to operate.
Only Saratoga and Pimlico predate it. It was in the Louisiana
Derby in 1924 that Black Gold launched its derby victory string
which included the golden jubilee Kentucky Derby at Churchill

Downs in Louisville. Black Gold is buried in the track's infield. The Fair Grounds traditionally opens each Thanksgiving and runs until spring. Jefferson Downs in Jefferson Parish operated for years but closed in 1992.

The largest crowds in the history of collegiate basketball watched the National Collegiate Athletic Association tournament in the Superdome in March of 1982. The games drew crowds ranging up to 61,612, and because of this the NCAA decided to hold the 1987 playoffs in the Dome.

New Orleans has had professional basketball franchises in the American Basketball Association from 1967 to 1970 and in the National Basketball Association from 1974 to 1979. Neither team was a winner, but the NBA entry, the Jazz, set the NBA attendance record with 35,077 in a game with the Philadelphia 76ers on November 30, 1977.

The Southern Yacht Club, situated on Lake Pontchartrain at West End, was founded in 1849 and is the second oldest in the United States, behind New York. Skippers representing the club have won two Olympic medals. Gilbert T. Gray won in the star class in 1932 and G. S. ("Buddy") Friedrichs, Jr., won in the dragon class in 1968.

New Orleans has had a major golf tournament for many years. It is now known as the Compaq Classic of New Orleans and is played at the English Turn Golf and Country Club in early May. It attracts annually many of the top touring PGA golfers.

The New Orleans Lawn Tennis Club, founded in 1890, is the oldest in the nation. Tulane University held the spotlight in collegiate tennis in the 1930s through the 1950s with teams developed by coaches Mercer Beasley and Emmett Paré. Seventeen of Beasley's players won eighty-four national titles, the stars of that era including Frankie Parker and Cliff Sutter. In twenty-six years at Tulane, Paré's teams won the Southeastern Conference championship eighteen times. Stars of the Paré teams were Ernie Sutter, Earl Bartlett, Les Longshore, Jack Tuero, Wade Herren, Hamilton Richardson, Jose Aguero, Ron Holmberg, and Crawford Henry.

Several women are among area athletes who have won national

recognition. Linda Tuero of Tulane won the U.S. Women's Open National Clay Courts tennis championship in 1970 and the National Women's Amateur tourneys in 1969 and 1970. Ranked nationally for seven years, she stood number ten in the world in 1972. Pam Jiles of Dillard University was a member of the Olympic 1,600-meter relay team; Mary Ann Villegas of Dominican College won the national intercollegiate women's golf championship in 1952; and Marion Turpie Lake won the women's Southern and Trans-Mississippi golf championships in 1926, and the Eastern crown in 1937.

Great athletes who developed in New Orleans include Mel Ott of Gretna, who became a member of the New York Giants baseball team at age seventeen; Emmett Toppino of Loyola, who was a 1932 Olympic gold medalist in the 400-meter relay; Mel Parnell, a leading pitcher for the Boston Red Sox for ten years; Pete Maravich, a former LSU star who became leading scorer with the Jazz in 1977; and Eddie Price, a 1949 All-America fullback at Tulane who starred later for the NFL Giants.

At the outset of the twenty-first century, Saints owner Tom Benson demanded that the state of Louisiana, owner of the Superdome, either update its seating configuration or provide a new stadium. The state named a committee to study the issue, with a view toward resolving it by 2008. Reengineering the Superdome remained a possibility, as did the Saints' departure from New Orleans by 2003 if improvements were not forthcoming.

W.G.C.

BIBLIOGRAPHY

Daily Herald, Biloxi-Gulfport, Miss., September 9, 1964.

Howard-Tilton Memorial Library, Special Collections, Louisiana Division, Tulane University

New Orleans *States,* March 25, 1954.

New Orleans *States-Item,* May 18, 1962; May 8, June 27, 1963; June 9, 1967; June 6, 1977 (Centennial Edition).

New Orleans *Times-Picayune,* July 18, 1957.

Tulane University Sports Publicity Department records.

27.

 THINGS TO DO AND SEE

The French Quarter holds the greatest interest for visitors, but there are many other things to see in New Orleans. A good place to start a tour of the Quarter is at the old Bank of Louisiana building, 334 Royal Street. This fine old structure dates back to 1826, and now houses the Greater New Orleans Tourist and Convention Commission. Here visitors may obtain maps and brochures about New Orleans, and view on the walls a pictorial history of the city.

Jackson Square commands the greatest attention, and this area should be at the top of any visitor's "must see" list. There are seven major attractions within a block of each other, all open to visitors.

The Square itself. View the majestic equestrian statue of General Andrew Jackson.

St. Louis Cathedral. The third church on the site, the cathedral was built in 1851. Guided tours are available.

The Cabildo. Built in 1795, the Cabildo is part of the Louisiana State Museum complex. It was here that the transfer of Louisiana from Spain to France took place on November 30, 1803, and twenty days later, the transfer from France to the United States. Open Tuesday–Sunday, 9–5. Fee.

The Presbytère. Begun in 1795, this building did not attain its present status until 1847. It was built as a residence for the clergy who served the cathedral. It is part of the Louisiana State Museum. Open Tuesday–Sunday, 9–5. Fee.

The Pontalba Buildings. Built for Micaela Almonester, Baroness Pontalba, in 1850, they were not, as is often erroneously stated, the first apartment houses in the United States. They are composed of row houses. The cast-iron work on the balconies is perhaps the finest in New Orleans. It features a medallion, at regular spaces, with the initials *A* and *P*, for Almonester and Pontalba.

The 1850 House. Situated in the Lower Pontalba Building, it reflects the way of life in a Creole family during the mid-nineteenth century. Open Tuesday–Sunday, 9–5. Fee.

The Moon Walk. The best place in town for a closeup view of what goes on in the river. Tugboats and ocean-going ships move up and down the channel and along the docks in a panorama of activity. Visitors may also get an overview of Jackson Square from atop the levee, where bleacher-type seats have been provided. Take it all in—free.

There are other "musts" in the Quarter, including:

Madame John's Legacy, 632 Dumaine Street. Built after 1788, this is an excellent example of French Colonial architecture, although it was constructed during the Spanish regime. The original house at this site was destroyed by fire. Part of Louisiana State Museum complex, and sometimes open to the public. Fee.

Gallier House, 1132 Royal Street. Erected in 1857 by James Gallier, Jr., noted New Orleans architect, for his own residence, this is a showplace of mid-nineteenth-century furnishings. Open Monday–Saturday, 10–5. Fee.

Beauregard House, 1113 Chartres Street. This house built in 1826 for Joseph Le Carpentier, grandfather of the famous chess player Paul Morphy, gets its name from the fact that Confederate General P. G. T. Beauregard lived here briefly after the Civil War. It was the winter home for many years of Frances Parkinson Keyes, the novelist, who deeded it to Keyes Foundation. Open Monday–Saturday, 10–3. Fee.

Ursuline Convent, 1100 Chartres Street. This is believed to be the oldest building in the Mississippi Valley. It was completed about 1750 and is considered one of the finest examples of French

Two miles above the Garden District, Audubon Park has on its 280 acres the zoo, one of the finest in the country, a golf course, and an aquarium. Photo by A. J. Meek.

Colonial architecture in existence. Public tours each Wednesday, 1:30 and 3:00 P.M. Fee.

Old U.S. Mint, corner of Decatur Street and Esplanade Avenue. This regional mint at one time produced $5 million a month in coins. It is now part of the Louisiana State Museum complex, housing a library and exhibits. Open Tuesday–Sunday, 9–5. Fee.

Hermann-Grima House, 820 St. Louis Street. Erected in 1831, this stately mansion, with a superb rear courtyard and garden, is furnished in the style of the mid-nineteenth century. It has been faithfully restored to its original splendor by the Christian Woman's Exchange. Open daily except Wednesday, 10–5; Sunday, 1–5. Fee.

Historic New Orleans Collection, 529–33 Royal Street. The Merieult House, a fine mansion built in 1792 and survivor of the fire of 1794, is now a museum which contains a rich store of documents, maps, prints, paintings, and books concerning New Orleans and Louisiana. Front exhibit hall, open to public, free; fee for tour of entire museum.

Musée Conti—Historical Wax Museum, 917 Conti Street. History of New Orleans and Louisiana Territory depicted in 144 life-size figures. Open daily, 10:00–5:30. Fee.

Superdome tour. Monday–Friday, 9:30–4:00. Fee.

Audubon Park Zoo. Renovated and expanded, this is regarded as one of the finest zoos in the nation. Animals may be seen from newly constructed walkways and paths which permit easy viewing. There is also a petting section, supervised. Open daily. Fee (except for senior citizens, who are admitted free).

New Orleans Museum of Art, in City Park. Permanent collections include art of Western civilization from the pre-Christian era to the present, plus the art of pre-Columbian America, Africa, and the Far East. Traveling exhibitions. Open Tuesday–Sunday, 10–5. Fee.

Confederate Museum, 929 Camp Street. Collection of material on the Civil War. Open Monday–Saturday, 10–4. Fee.

Chalmette National Battlefield Park, St. Bernard Parish. National cemetery, plus famous Pakenham oaks and park grounds, information on the Battle of New Orleans. Open daily, 7–6. Free.

Longue Vue Gardens, 7 Bamboo Road. Elegant home furnished with eighteenth- and nintheenth-century antiques surrounded with beautiful gardens covering seven acres. Open Tuesday–Friday, 10–4:30; Saturday and Sunday, 1–5. Fee.

Louisiana Nature Center, 11000 Lake Forest Boulevard, in East New Orleans. Eighty-six acres of nature trails, nature preserve, and exhibit hall showing Louisiana's natural environment. Open Tuesday–Friday, 9–5; Saturday and Sunday, 12–5. Fee.

Riverboats. The *Natchez,* the *John J. Audubon,* and the *Creole Queen* offer trips on the Mississippi River from the New Orleans docks, and the *Audubon* offers round-trip service to the Audubon Zoo. Check their telephone listings for time schedules and fares.

Aquarium of the Americas, at the foot of Canal Street and the river. A fantastic display of many species of fish and sea animals. Fee.

Entergy Imax Theater, adjacent to the aquarium. Big-screen spectacles. Fee.

Audubon Living Science Museum, Custom House on Canal Street, opening in 2001. Fee.

Woldenberg Park, alongside river from the aquarium to Jackson Square area. Delightful place to relax and view river activity. Free.

Mardi Gras Museum, at the Presbytere on Jackson Square. A collection of Carnival memorabilia, including costumes and decorations. Fee.

D-Day Museum, in the Warehouse District. An exhibit commemorating the United States' part in World War II, including the Normandy invasion of June 6, 1944. This museum quickly drew national attention. Fee.

Odgen Museum of Southern Art, at Lee Circle. An exhibit of the visual arts of the South. Fee.

Jazzland, in eastern New Orleans. A popular theme park offering thrilling rides and shows for children and adults, plus theater and food. Fee.

Children's Museum, at 420 Julia Street. Plenty of things for children to do and see. Fee.

Preservation Hall, at 726 St. Peter Street in the French Quarter. Jazz played by the old masters. Fee.

Garden District tour. See pages 55–61.

Cemeteries tour. See pages 62–80.

Streetcar ride. See page 265.

Free ferry ride. Board at Canal Street and the river.

New Orleans has become a city of festivals, and some of them draw national, even international, attention. The major festivals include:

Mardi Gras, held on movable dates. See chart on page 186.

Jazz and Heritage Festival, held at the Fair Grounds race track in late April and early May. Jazz, Cajun, gospel music, and food abound. Fee.

French Quarter Festival, held on streets and in nightclubs of French Quarter in mid-April. Features jazz, parades, and food.

Spring Fiesta, held in late March and early April. Begins with a presentation of queen and court in Jackson Square and a parade in the Quarter. Continues over two weekends, with tours of historic homes. Fee.

Essence Music Festival, held first weekend of July in the Superdome, with programs by African American musicians and performers. Fee.

Tennessee Williams/New Orleans Literary Festival, held in early Spring, with accent on history and the arts. Fee.

Black Heritage Festival, held in early March at Armstrong Park, New Orleans Museum of Art, and Louisiana State Museum, in honor of African Americans. Fee.

New Orleans Film and Video Festival, held each fall at various locations. Fee.

For specific information on events, contact the New Orleans Metropolitan Convention and Visitor's Bureau at 1-504-566-5011. FAX 1-504-566-5021.

W.G.C.

❧ SUMMING UP ❧

New Orleanians have been accused of smugly sitting back and cherishing their heritage while other cities in the South were racing full stride through the twentieth century. There is a germ of truth in the slander; otherwise, why would the exotic city on the Mississippi be a Mecca for vacationers and convention-goers?

They come to share, if even for a fleeting moment, a way of life, to savor an "eat, drink, and be merry" style adopted by a population that learned to dance and sing its way through adversity, that took time to smell the roses. They come to feast, to tap their toes to the two-beat. Most of all, they are drawn by a feeling of nostalgia, a yearning to revisit the past through links that are unique to New Orleans: the French Quarter, the gaslight-era street lamps, the paddle-wheel boats on the river, the horse-drawn buggies going past iron-lace balconies.

Only now, as the city moves into a new century, is Bienville's capital regaining the momentum that carried it to prosperity and preeminence in the heady era before the cannon roared at Bull Run. Paradoxically, the renaissance is based partly on the hedonistic pleasures that New Orleanians insisted on enjoying while the puritan ethic, and a desire to get rich, was driving the people of other southern centers to surpass the old Louisiana town in population and business activity. It is the tourists attracted by the city's reputation for fun who have added thousands of new jobs to the economy, impelled investors to build the hotels that have transformed the Central Business District.

Atlanta, Columbia, and Jackson were burned by invading armies, but of all the towns in the Confederacy, New Orleans suffered the most economically because of the Civil War and the trade-stifling Reconstruction. Once the shooting was over, railroads quickly crisscrossed the continent and usurped the cargoes of the steamboats that had made New Orleans the busiest port in the nation. The political unrest of the carpetbag times was a factor in the sidetracking of the city when the rail network was being expanded.

Millions of bales of cotton were toted over the levee, bound for Europe or the northeastern United States, where coal and milldams provided the power for textile plants. The cotton could have been processed on the riverbank, creating a manufacturing boom of historic proportions, except that the machinery which could be powered by oil or gas had not been invented—and anyway, nobody knew of the fossil riches that lay underground in Louisiana. Until 1905, recurrent yellow fever epidemics ravaged the city, resulting in embargoes that were ruinous to business people.

By the time the petroleum reserves of Louisiana began to be tapped, Houston, Dallas, and other southwestern cities already had a head start because of the fabulous Texas fields that gushed forth earlier, coincident with the mass production of automobiles. Even so, New Orleans remained the largest metropolis in the South until World War II. Afterwards, geography worked to the advantage of other cities. Atlanta was strategically situated to become the hub of the South's air routes, and Miami (any map of the Western Hemisphere shows why) grew into the aviation gateway of the Americas.

Mardi Gras, debutante seasons, opera, symphony, fishing, golf, cards, dinners, and club functions notwithstanding—all play and no work mean the poorhouse—the city's employers have provided jobs for a growing metropolitan population. The port has remained first or second in the United States (depending on the measurement used), thanks in part to the development of the inland waterway system and the proliferation of barge traffic. Ironically, the barges have taken some of the volume from the railroads that originally doomed the steamboats by siphoning away their lifeblood. The new office buildings attest to the city's emergence as an oil industry center keyed to the great offshore exploration and production boom. And the complex of petroleum and chemical plants that stretches along the shores of the Mississippi all the way to Baton Rouge is further evidence of economic vitality.

How is a city judged? By its per capita income, its number of households, its bank clearings? Or is there another, and perhaps even more persuasive criterion: Do its inhabitants enjoy life? New Orleanians do.

It may be not only the activities themselves—the eating, drinking, playing—that are conducive to pleasure but also the setting itself, the ambience, the environment, the surroundings. Very early, New Orleans had its hours of glory or of despair. As a result its people have a highly developed sense of history. Because they do, the preservationists prevailed, and now the French Quarter, the Garden District, and other older neighborhoods provide a continuity with the past that residents find both comfortable and stimulating, and so do visitors.

Remember? We told you New Orleans is different.

J.W.

LAGNIAPPE

Lottery

"The first thing that strikes the attention of the stranger visiting New Orleans is the all pervading character of the Louisiana Lottery Company. It has become almost a part of the city; its tickets are for sale in, we may say, thousands of windows. Its power and its influence are felt everywhere." Thus in 1880 did the *Daily States* describe a gambling phenomenon unequaled in this country until the gaudy casinos sprang up in Las Vegas, Reno, and Atlantic City in the present century and until sovereign states began augmenting their tax revenues with lotteries offering million-dollar prizes.

In the twenty-five years from 1868 until 1893, it was easier to buy a lottery ticket in New Orleans than a loaf of bread. Almost every city square had its lottery shop. And in its time, the lottery was big business, payoffs on a single drawing running to $300,000. Everything was computed in boxcar figures. The company netted more than $1 million a month. And the bribes paid to legislators for a monopoly charter totaled $300,000, according to an affidavit by one of the founders. As visible as the lottery was in the city, only 7 percent of the revenues came from Louisianians. The rest poured in through the mails from the rest of the country. Every state in the Union made its contribution.

The Louisiana State Lottery Company had its headquarters in its own building at St. Charles and Union streets. Periodic drawings were held in a theater across the street. The awards were scrupulously honest. In order to assure public confidence, the lottery engaged Confederate Generals P. G. T. Beauregard, a New Orleans war hero, and Jubal A. Early of Virginia to preside as the numbers were lifted from drums by blindfolded boys.

Campaigning for a renewal of its charter, the company courted good will by spending thousands of dollars on public projects. In 1890, President M. A. Dauphin wrote a $50,000 check to pay the wages of workers hired by the city to combat a flood. The lottery also spent hundreds of thousands of dollars on advertising to influence newspapers.

With the exception of race, no issue since the Civil War has been as divisive in Louisiana as was the attempt of the company in 1890 to win an extended franchise. The Anti-Lottery League began publishing a daily newspaper, the *New Delta*, to counter the editorials of publishers who had succumbed to the lottery's largesse.

The company managed to get the Louisiana Legislature to submit the proposed renewal to the electorate, and on March 22, 1892, the vote against the lottery was 157,422 to 4,225. But the operation already was doomed by the passage by Congress of a law forbidding the shipment of lottery material in the mails. The last drawing was held in New Orleans in December, 1892. For a few months the lottery was operated in Spanish Honduras, but a crackdown on agents in the United States was the last straw.

While the lottery was officially ended, gambling remained in the New Orleans area through the early part of the twentieth century through the operation of gambling houses in parishes adjacent to New Orleans. And the lottery continued in New Orleans on an illicit basis, with drawings held on the run; that is, in different locations. This continued until Mayor Morrison came into office in 1946.

In 1992 a new Louisiana lottery was born, sanctioned by the legislature, with twice-weekly drawings. The legislature also authorized more than a dozen casinos, four in the New Orleans area. These include Harrah's, at the foot of Canal Street near the river; Bally's, at Southshore Harbor in New Orleans, the Treasure Chest in Kenner, and Boomtown in Gretna.

This monument, which stands near the entrance to Greenwood Cemetery, memorializes the Benevolent Protective Order of Elks. Photo by A. J. Meek.

Roulette wheels and slot machines whiz and dice roll to the tune of millions of dollars in revenue for the city of New Orleans and the state, and hometowners and visitors who indulge satisfy their cravings. Harrah's, announcing it was threatened with bankruptcy because of what it claimed were exorbitant taxes, won relief in a session of the legislature in 2001.

J . W .

Monuments

The warriors predominate among the monuments with which New Orleans pays homage to heroes of the past, but the founder of the city and a freehearted Irish woman immigrant also get their due. As in European capitals, scores of statues dot the cityscape, a few of them landmarks and all of them history lessons for residents and visitors alike.

Oddly perhaps, the most prominent monument honors a man who set foot in the city, if at all, only en route to or from the war in Mexico or military stations in Texas. But Robert E. Lee did command New Orleans units that were part of his Army of Northern Virginia, and the principal general of the Confederacy was not forgotten in the flood of sentiment that engulfed the South in the years following the Civil War.

A statue of Lee stands atop a column in Lee Circle, at St. Charles Avenue and Howard Avenue, the top of his head a full 109 feet above ground level. He looks down St. Charles toward Canal Street, facing north, of course, because, New Orleanians explain, Lee would never turn his back on the Yankees.

Lee's daughters, Mildred and Mary, participated in the unveiling ceremonies on Washington's Birthday, 1884. The sixteen-and-a-half-foot bronze statue was designed by sculptor Alexander Doyle. The Lee Circle area seemed forlorn throughout the year of 1953 because the monument had to be dismantled while rotting foundation pilings were replaced. Residents greeted the return of a familiar figure on January 19, 1954, when the work was completed.

Equally well known is Clark Mills's equestrian statue of Andrew Jackson, the savior of New Orleans, in Jackson Square. The park-like area still was known as the Place d'Armes on January 13, 1840, when the general himself laid the cornerstone, twenty-five years after his ragtag army defeated the British invaders in the Battle of New Orleans. The statue was unveiled in 1856.

In 1862, General Benjamin F. Butler, leader of the Federal troops occupying the captured city, had Jackson's own words engraved in the base of the monument. "The Union Must and Shall be Preserved," says the inscription, not very apt at the time as far as most of the Rebel-minded citizens were concerned.

The statue has a familiar look to visitors from Washington, D.C., and Nashville, Tennessee, where replicas of Mills's work stand. He made three castings. Some years ago pranksters invaded Jackson Square one night and stole the statue's head. Later, others made off with Jackson's sword. The head was recovered undamaged and the sword replaced.

Another Civil War general whose monument adorns the scene is New Orleans' own Pierre Gustave Toutant Beauregard. A bronze equestrian statue by Alexander Doyle has stood since 1915 at an entrance to City Park, where Esplanade Avenue crosses Bayou St.

John. Beauregard, who directed the firing on Fort Sumter at the beginning of the war, was in command at the Battle of Shiloh after Albert Sidney Johnston's death and was one of the Confederacy's four-star generals. He returned to New Orleans after the war and was active in civic affairs until his death in 1893.

Two days after the White League defeated the carpetbag government's Metropolitan Police and militia in the Battle of Liberty Place on September 14, 1874, the *Daily Picayune* called for the erection of a memorial to the white citizens who died in the outbreak. The cornerstone for a monument was laid on September 14, 1891, in the median of Canal Street near the Mississippi River. Eventually it interfered with traffic and was moved. The monument provoked controversy during the civil rights movement of the 1960s because it hailed advocates of white supremacy.

On Loyola Avenue at Howard Avenue, near the entrance to the Union Passenger Terminal, the city unveiled on April 24, 1955, a statue designed by sculptor Angela Gregory in honor of Jean-Baptiste Le Moyne, Sieur de Bienville, who chose the site for New Orleans and ordered the establishment of a capital of the French territory of Louisiana.

Alexander Doyle was the designer of an imposing statue at Margaret Place, where Camp, Prytania, and Clio streets meet. It has the simple inscription "Margaret" and is a memorial to Margaret Gaffney Haughery. The Irish-born woman, who operated a bakery, won the hearts of New Orleanians with her gifts to the poor and her work on behalf of sufferers during the yellow fever epidemics of the nineteenth century. In 1884, when the statue was erected, everybody knew who "Margaret" was.

Joel Hart's statue of statesman Henry Clay, unveiled on April 12, 1860, in the median of Canal Street at St. Charles, stood in a small circle around which two historic mass meetings were held. One preceded the Battle of Liberty Place on September 14, 1874, and the other was the rallying point for the mob that marched to the parish prison on March 15, 1891, and killed eleven Sicilians accused of assassinating the police superintendent. The statue ent. The statue was moved in 1900 to Lafayette Square, opposite Gallier Hall, then the City Hall.

Many other monuments also mark the New Orleans scene. These include Confederate President Jefferson Davis, Confederate Generals Stonewall Jackson, Albert Sidney Johnston, and Albert Pike, South American patriot Simón Bolívar, nineteenth-century philanthropist John McDonogh, and U.S. Senator and Chief Justice Edward Douglass White.

J.W.

BIBLIOGRAPHY

Cocke, Edward J. *Monumental New Orleans*. New Orleans, 1968.

Laffite

The role of Jean Laffite, pirate or smuggler, in the Battle of New Orleans has been greatly publicized and romanticized. Some of the publicity would have you believe that he, and not General Andrew Jackson, was the real hero.

When British Admiral Sir Alexander Cochrane's fleet of more than fifty vessels with 7,500 redcoats aboard appeared at the mouth of Lake Borgne in 1814, Laffite offered his band of smugglers in the defense of New Orleans; and General Jackson accepted. Laffite, familiar with the bayous because he was headquartered at Grand Terre Isle, south of Barataria Bay, supplied his knowledge of the area, and flints for some of Jackson's flintlock rifles. Laffite's Baratarians manned two batteries in the Battle of New Orleans, with the picturesque Dominique You and René Beluche as cannoneers.

The fact is that neither Jean nor his brother Pierre was in the battle lines at Chalmette. He and his brother are supposed to have been defending one of the swampy approaches to New Orleans.

Governor Claiborne of Louisiana had put a price on Laffite's head because of his smuggling activities. How much help he gave Jackson has been a matter of conjecture since the battle. Over the years, Jean Laffite has become a legend, so much so that even his blacksmith shop at 941 Bourbon Street is a tourist spot. At least it could have been his blacksmith shop, if he had had one.

J.C.C.

Duels

Governor W. C. C. Claiborne of the Territory of Orleans received a wound in the thigh on June 8, 1807, in a pistol duel with Daniel Clark, a wealthy Irishman who aspired to the post to which Claiborne had been appointed by President Thomas Jefferson.

Their encounter near Fort Manchac was the first notable affair of honor in a century in which hot-blooded Creoles and brawling Americans alike sought satisfaction with swords or pistols in secluded spots in the New Orleans area. In 1839 the *Daily Picayune* commented that duels were "as common these days as watermelons."

Too often there was an empty seat for the homeward drive in one of the carriages that took the antagonists to the rendezvous arranged by punctilious seconds after a real or fancied insult resulted in a challenge. Sometimes a pin prick that brought a drop of blood in a sword fight fulfilled the conditions of the code, and the combatants shook hands. Frequently, both missed with their first shots when pistols were used to settle the issue, and both were willing to be friends. But not always. It was the battles to the death, or the threat of them, that finally caused a revulsion of feeling against an uncivilized practice, and ended duels in the final years of the nineteenth century. The meetings always had been forbidden by law and interdicted by the Church, but only the force of public opinion finally induced prickly tempered New Orleanians to give up an opportunity to kill their enemies and resort to fist fights or court suits instead.

In colonial times the Creoles duelled with the rapier or colichemarde, a sword with a sharp-pointed triangular blade. The Americans who poured in after the Louisiana Purchase favored the pistol, and in time the Creoles, too, began to choose the firearm. Popular duelling grounds were the garden behind the St. Louis Cathedral, where blades sometimes flashed in the moonlight, a stand of oak trees in City Park, and a field beside the slaughterhouse near the river in St. Bernard Parish.

The strictest protocol governed the delivery of a challenge, the acceptance, and the conduct of the combatants in the duel itself. The guidelines were passed down by word of mouth until Don Jose Quintero drew up *The Code of Honor* in 1866. Legend has it that proceedings were not always as gentlemanly as the rules would suggest. It is said that more than one citizen who wanted to dispose of an enemy hired a professional fencing master to make up a pretext, deliver a challenge, and dispatch the unfortunate foe.

Best known of the New Orleans masters was Pepe Llulla (pronounced "yu-ya"), a student of the famed L'Alouette. Llulla, a dead-eye pistol shot as well as an unbeatable swordsman, fought at least twenty duels in the middle years of the nineteenth century, and was a second on countless occasions. He once purchased his own cemetery, but indignantly protested that he did not intend to fill it with his own victims.

Newspaper editors in an era when writing was vitriolic and insults regularly delivered in print figured in several New Orleans duels. A surgeon, Dr. Thomas Hunt, killed John Frost, editor of the *Crescent*, in 1851. After a bloodless encounter in 1880 between E. A. Burke, managing editor of the *Times-Democrat*, and Henry J. Hearsey, editor of the *Daily States*, Mark Bigney, editor of the *Daily City Item*, reflected in an editorial the rising public opposition to duelling. He wrote: "We understand it to be the intent of some of our legislators to so amend the duelling laws as to protect duels from police interference; to make it an imperative condition of all such meetings that the fight must continue until one or both are killed, and to hold the survivor, in case there be one, to a rigid accountability for the blood he sheds. This would give an air of serious solemnity to such affairs of honor."

J.W.

BIBLIOGRAPHY

Kane, Harnett T. *Gentlemen, Swords and Pistols*. New York, 1951.
Wilds, John. *Afternoon Story*. Baton Rouge, 1977.

Streetcars

New Orleans has had public transportation in one form or another since 1835. One major streetcar line still operates on St. Charles and Carrollton Avenues, from Canal Street looping Uptown to Claiborne Avenue—and the Canal streetcar line, discontinued in 1964, is scheduled to start up again during 2003. There is also a riverside line that runs from the intersection of Canal Street and the river to Esplanade Avenue.

The first public transportation in the city used mule-drawn omnibuses, which were succeeded by steam-powered railcars. Later came horses and mule cars pulled on rails.

Electric streetcars debuted on February 1, 1893, and for many years served the entire city. The St. Charles line has been placed on the National Register of Historic Places. Besides being a tourist attraction, the St. Charles line carries thousands of residents to and from the business district daily.

W.G.C.

Sin

Storyville's name has survived in infamy, but the notorious red-light district was only a tea party in comparison to two New Orleans sin spots that earlier set Western Hemisphere standards for lawlessness, for rowdiness, for sheer depravity.

The St. Charles is the oldest streetcar line in continuous operation in the world and is included in the National Register of Historic Places. It's a wonderful way to see the uptown area of the city. Photo by A. J. Meek.

Neither Sodom nor Gomorrah offered baser pleasures than those provided for Mississippi River flatboatmen in the first part of the nineteenth century by the Swamp, and for rivermen, sailors, and rural carousers in the latter half of the 1800s by Gallatin Street.

A discussion of the seamy side of New Orleans must begin with Storyville because of the district's visibility, and because the association of the bordellos with the development of Dixieland jazz has left the memories of the area partly obscured by a romantic fog.

The beginning came in 1897. A respectable city councilman, Sidney Story, outraged because houses of prostitution were operating in the French Quarter and salesladies in Canal Street stores could look out the rear windows and see "scenes that would make a man blush for shame," introduced a control ordinance. The council adopted his measure, which did not legitimatize prostitution, but forbade the practice anywhere except in an area bounded by Basin, Iberville, North Robertson, and St. Louis streets.

Prostitutes, madams, and pimps took over. Hundreds of prostitutes, white and black, established themselves in the district. In front, along Basin Street, were veritable mansions. To the rear stretched rows of ramshackle, one-room cribs. Leaning out of windows, the women tried to entice passers-by. One ploy was to grab a man's hat, and he had to go inside to recover it. The going price for a sexual encounter was a dollar. In the big Basin Street houses, where an air of elegance was maintained and champagne flowed, small groups provided music, much of which took on the jazz two-beat. To the city councilman's distress, the district became known as Storyville.

For twenty years Storyville roared from dusk to dawn. The end came on November 12, 1917. Military authorities in Washington, concerned about the effects on the morals of young soldiers and sailors training for action in the First World War, demanded the closing of the district. Mayor Martin Behrman, who believed prostitution could only be controlled by sequestering it, reluctantly complied. As Behrman expected, the Storyville women scattered over the city and continued their activities clandestinely. There is scarcely a trace of Storyville remaining today. Most of the area now is occupied by a government housing project.

After the Louisiana Purchase in 1803, rough-and-ready frontiersmen began floating goods down the Mississippi to New Orleans in flatboats. They arrived with money in their pockets and an urge for wine and women, never mind the song. They headed for the Swamp, a collection of hovels on Girod Street, an area very close to the present Louisiana Superdome. It was, said Herbert Asbury in *The French Quarter*, the "toughest, most vicious area that ever flourished in the United States." It also was the crudest, physically. The shacks that served as saloons, bordellos, gambling dens, and flophouses were built of cypress planks and wood from flatboats that were broken up once a journey was completed. A partition divided most shacks into two rooms. In the front was a bar, sometimes merely a plank laid across two kegs. In the rear were gambling tables and cubicles where prostitutes earned their living. Covering the windows were red curtains, behind which red lanterns were lit, as though it were necessary to advertise the nature of such an establishment.

Robberies, assaults, and brawls went on around the clock, and Asbury wrote that murders averaged half a dozen a week, most of them unreported. Police feared to come near. For twenty years, it was said, no officer set foot in the Swamp. Gangs that operated out of the area preyed on the city. One ploy was to set fire to a house, and loot it during the excitement. In 1828, authorities got word of and nipped a plot to burn the whole city.

By the time of the Civil War the Swamp was being eclipsed by Gallatin Street, a two-block stretch that no longer exists because of changes on the riverfront, but which was in the French Quarter area between the French Market and the United States Mint. Gallatin Street was a row of barrelhouses—all a man could drink for five cents—bordellos, dance houses, gin mills, and sailors' boardinghouses. In the daytime the establishments were shuttered, and at night they came alive. Sometimes police would team up for a daylight foray, but at night they stayed away.

The prostitutes had to be able to kick and gouge in a brawl, or

A PEACEFUL EVENING ON GALLATIN STREET

During the Civil War era, this two-block stretch of Gallatin Street (which no longer exists) in the Vieux Carré was a center of rampant vice. It was so dangerous at night that the police stayed away. The Historic New Orleans Collection.

they'd never last. The street was terrorized by the Live Oak Boys, a gang founded in 1858 by Red Bill Wilson, who cracked heads with their oak cudgels. Sometimes the gang raided a dance hall. Customers and prostitutes would flee through rear doors and windows, and the Live Oak Boys then wrecked the premises.

Among the perils that awaited a sailor or farmer venturing into Gallatin Street was the chance of being shanghaied, although mere robbery was much more common. The girls used to dance in one-piece dresses, wearing nothing underneath. Sometimes they got carried away and shook off the dresses. Their dancing partners might respond by peeling off their own clothing. On Gallatin Street, anything went.

J.W.

BIBLIOGRAPHY

Asbury, Herbert. *The French Quarter*. New York, 1936.

The Port

New Orleans' port, the real reason the city was built, ranks as the world's busiest, with more than 6,000 ships and other vessels moving through it annually on the Mississippi River. In terms of ranking in the United States, it is always at or near the top, providing more than 90,000 jobs directly related to maritime activity.

As the port entered the twenty-first century, it had become strongly market oriented, the premier port in the nation in the handling of coffee, steel, and rubber. By the latter part of the previous century, development of special niches had built its general cargo measurably in the import and export of drywall and plywood.

One of its principal exports is grain, which floats down in barges from points in the Midwest. A Foreign Trade Zone, in operation since shortly after World War II, permits merchandise to be brought into the United States without being immediately subject to Customs regulations.

Cruise ships carry approximately a half-million persons to destinations in the Caribbean and Mexico on weekly sailings. And there are excursions along the Mississippi and Ohio rivers that originate in New Orleans.

Hurricanes and Climate

Sitting as it does nearly one hundred miles from the Gulf of Mexico, New Orleans (as well as its environs—principally St. Bernard, Plaquemines, and Jefferson parishes) at times finds itself in the path of devastating hurricanes.

From the middle of the twentieth century until its end, the city felt the brunt of three major hurricanes, each inflicting multimillion-dollar damages. One in 1947, prior to the time hurricanes were given names, flooded the lower part of the city, along with parts of St. Bernard and Plaquemines parishes. Hurricane Betsy in 1965 also struck the lower regions with high water and damaging gusts, and in 1969 the city and region felt the fierce winds and rainfall caused by Hurricane Camille, whose main target was the Mississippi Gulf Coast, where it left stretches of the coast in shambles.

Modern weather forecasting methods have lessened the threats of hurricanes, giving residents time to prepare.

The New Orleans area has generally mild weather with frequent rains. Temperatures range into the upper 90s during the summer, with the hottest recorded day being June 22, 1915, when the mercury reached 102.2 degrees Fahrenheit, and into freezing in the winter, with temperatures dipping into the 20s and even lower at times. Cold spells usually are of short duration, but lows in the teens and below do occur, though infrequently.

Annual rainfall measures in the 60s generally. On the wettest day recorded, April 15–16, 1927, 14.01 inches of rain fell; and coldest day recorded, February 13, 1899, reached 6.8 degrees Fahrenheit. Snowfalls are rare, the greatest being one on January 14–15, 1895, measuring 8.2 inches.

Figures courtesy of Nash C. Roberts, Jr., weather consultant.

❧ ABOUT THE AUTHORS ❧

JOHN C. CHASE, cartoonist, author, historian, humorist, and witty authority on New Orleans, began editorial cartooning in the turbulent Huey P. Long era, worked for both New Orleans afternoon dailies, then at WDSU-TV, where he originated the television editorial cartoon. His classic, *Frenchmen, Desire, Good Children and Other Streets of New Orleans,* is still a best seller. His *Louisiana Purchase* was a popular cartoon history. He was a past president of the Association of Editorial Cartoonists, a founding member of National Cartoonists Society, International House, and the Escargot Gourmet Society. He died in 1986.

WALTER G. COWAN, retired editor of the New Orleans *States-Item,* began his career as a reporter on the old New Orleans *Item.* A graduate of Mississippi Gulf Coast Junior College and the University of Missouri, he was also a vice-president of the Times-Picayune Publishing Corporation. After retiring, he taught journalism at the University of New Orleans. He coauthored this book and *Louisiana Yesterday and Today.*

CHARLES L. DUFOUR, a native of New Orleans, was a graduate of Tulane, which awarded him an honorary doctorate in 1978. He died in 1996, on the eve of the publication of *Louisiana Yesterday and Today.* A leading Louisiana historian, he was a columnist for New Orleans newspapers and author of some twenty books.

O. K. LEBLANC, the originator of the idea for this book, graduated from Louisiana State University with a degree in journalism in 1939. From 1944–47 he was the editor and publisher of the *Marine Corps Gazette*. In World War II, he served as Company Commander of Marine Launchings at Guadalcanal, Tarawa, and Saipan, and retired from the service as a colonel in 1955. He is former director of public relations for Louisiana Power & Light and coauthored a history of that company. He is also the author of *Cajun Boy* (1993), his autobiography. He now works as a PR consultant.

JOHN WILDS, a former Associated Press bureau chief and later city editor and special writer for the *States-Item,* was also a correspondent for *Time, Life,* and *Sports Illustrated* magazines and author of *Afternoon Story,* the history of the *States-Item,* as well as coauthor of this book. He died in 1999.

An authors' gathering following publication of *New Orleans Yesterday and Today.* From left: Charles L. Dufour, O. K. LeBlanc, Walter G. Cowan, John Wilds, and John C. Chase. Courtesy of the *Times-Picayune*

✤ INDEX ✤